Beyond Belief

THE STORY OF DENYS EYRE BOWER

MARY ELDRIDGE

Elmside Publishing

© Copyright Mary Eldridge 1996

Cover design by Jemma Hatt

This book is licensed by the Intellectual Property Office. Licence number: OWLS000409 https://www.orphanworkslicensing.service.gov.uk/view-register/details?owlsNumber=OWLS000409-1&filter=0

ISBN: 978-1-916528-04-8

All views and opinions expressed by the author do not reflect those of the publisher. The publisher does not warrant the complete accuracy of the information contained in this text, and it should not be relied upon as such.

I should like to thank Sue Casson and Catherine Noden for helping to prepare the manuscript for publication and Ron and Rene Vernon for their general assistance.

Contents

Foreword — vii

Chapter 1	1
Chapter 2	9
Chapter 3	12
Chapter 4	15
Chapter 5	19
Chapter 6	22
Chapter 7	26
Chapter 8	29
Chapter 9	31
Chapter 10	35
Chapter 11	39
Chapter 12	42
Chapter 13	46
Chapter 14	50
Chapter 15	53
Chapter 16	56
Chapter 17	59
Chapter 18	62
Chapter 19	66
Chapter 20	69
Chapter 21	72
Chapter 22	79
Chapter 23	83
Chapter 24	86
Chapter 25	94
Chapter 26	99
Chapter 27	102
Chapter 28	105
Chapter 29	108
Chapter 30	110

Chapter 31	113
Chapter 32	120
Chapter 33	123
Chapter 34	126
Chapter 35	128
Chapter 36	130
Chapter 37	132
Chapter 38	134
Chapter 39	138
Chapter 40	140
Chapter 41	143
Chapter 42	145
Chapter 43	148
Chapter 44	151
Chapter 45	154
Chapter 46	156
Chapter 47	162
Chapter 48	164
Chapter 49	168
Chapter 50	170
Chapter 51	177
Chapter 52	183
Epilogue	185

Foreword

This is the story of Denys Eyre Bower and Chiddingstone Castle from the time we became associated with it in 1961.

One

It was Easter Sunday 1961, and it was raining. The guests at the little country house hotel deep in Herefordshire where my sister, Ruth, and I were staying for the holiday, had long since given up hope of diverting themselves in the sodden countryside, and had settled down in the comfortable lounge, reading the papers which our host had thoughtfully provided for us. That was why Ruth was reading the Sunday Pictorial - it was the only one left.

As she glanced through it she caught sight of a small paragraph nestling above an advertisement for Dad's Cookies. She handed it to me, saying "Do you remember that extraordinary case?" The paragraph announced curtly that Denys Bower was not in solitary confinement at Parkhurst Prison, as stated in a previous issue, but had never moved from Wormwood Scrubs, where he was still confined.

I did remember the drama of Denys Bower, THE cause celebre of the mid-fifties. So fantastic that for weeks it was the source of delicious titbits for the popular press - all suitably spiced up. Our paper being *The Times*, we got only the plain unvarnished truth, but that was startling enough. But most scandals are ephemera, forgotten as quickly as last night's dream. The reason Denys Bower's name had stuck in our minds was that we had actually had a slight acquaintance with him - he lived in the same neighbourhood. For us he really existed, and a more conventional person you could not hope to find- or so it had seemed.

We were therefore all the more astonished when we learned that Denys Bower had got himself into deep trouble, as a result of which he was later charged with attempted murder and suicide. It was alleged that he had - of malice aforethought - taken a pot shot at his ex-fiancée, who had jilted him, and then tried to kill himself.

Not a very original tragedy. It was the accompanying circumstances that were so bizarre. Probably it was this that delighted the Press; the case was not a bit sordid, more like a musical comedy plot, it could be served up to the most squeamish reader. No one remembered the suffering of the principal actor, Bower, who had critically injured himself (the lady, readers will be reassured to hear, was not seriously hurt and left hospital after a few days).

Bower strenuously denied the charge of attempted murder it was all an accident. Nevertheless the jury found him guilty and the judge sentenced him to life imprisonment, being, as he said, much impressed by the prison doctor's medical report. In prison Bower would receive the right sort of psychiatric treatment. Well, well, well. There was general, but quite mild, surprise at the sentence. Maybe the judge knew something awful which the public did not. And British justice cannot go wrong, can it...?

So Bower was effectively removed from society, but evidently was still providing fodder for the Sunday Pictorial. What was the story they had retracted? We had no idea.

We personally had been flabbergasted at the result of the trial. It seemed quite unjustified by the evidence, and was not in line with the sort of sentences then being given. Six months later, for instance, there was a horrible case: a man knifed his fiancée most brutally and he only got six months. We felt uneasy in our minds -

something had gone wrong, someone should do something about it - his friends or relations - perhaps it was only a token sentence, and the intention was to release him shortly. "I had no idea he was still inside", said Ruth. Having a little time on our hands, we sat there and reminisced.

Denys Bower and we were fairly near neighbours, for we both lived in St. Marylebone; he resided in style in one of the old houses in Portman Square, we in a more modest location, in a flat in Wimpole Street. My father and sister, solicitors, were partners, and we all - parents, sister and myself - shared a flat above the firm's

office. We came across Denys Bower at the inaugural meeting of the St. Marylebone Society, whose object was to record the Borough's distinguished past, and ensure that it had an equally brilliant future. The Society failed dismally in the latter object, for the borough was embraced by the octopus of Westminster, decanonised, and from being a lively community became a desert of offices and one-way streets.

But the audience that evening was full of hopes and plans. I remembered Denys Bower well: a handsome, well-set up man-about-town in his mid-thirties (in fact he was older), a person of some dignity and reserve. He did not talk a great deal, although he was well qualified to do so, for he had been secretary of the Derbyshire Archaeological Society, and was an authority on architecture and various branches of the fine arts.

After a short while he ceased to attend the meetings, and we never saw him again, though we often passed his antique shop in Baker Street, by Portman Square. It was always a pleasure to look at the window, full of interesting things and beautifully set out. It was so elegant we could never think of a reason for going in - a pity, for his prices were reasonable and he was kind to the amateur. His own personal collections were set out in his house in Portman Square. I daresay he would have let us see it, had we asked. In the mid-fifties, the inglorious redevelopment of Portman Square and Baker Street began. Denys Bower was turned out of home and shop. We missed the shop, but never wondered what had happened to the owner.

In fact he was facing a triple problem: he had to find a home for himself, his collections, and his business, and he solved it in a characteristically ingenious fashion. He bought a country mansion, Chiddingstone Castle in Kent, in easy reach of London, where he put his collections on view to the public. The entry fees were to

pay for running the house, where he could also do a little dealing.

It opened in May 1956, and why we never heard of it I do not know. For every weekend we made a trip out of London, searching out new places to explore.

As it was, we heard nothing about Denys Bower until September 1957. Then one morning, the news was on the front page of all the papers: Castle-owner shoots fiancée. The 'castle-owner' was Denys Bower. It was the popular Press which coined this term. I suppose it had a feudal ring, which made matters even more romantic than they were. We learned that he had become engaged to a young lady, some thirty years his junior, who had posed to him as the Comtesse d'Estainville, although she was really the daughter of a Peckham bus-driver (or cab-driver, the Press seemed uncertain about this).

One's first reaction to the headlines was that the outraged lover, on discovery of the truth, had taken his revenge. But no. The poor man had not known the truth when what was claimed was an accident happened. The lady's story was so fantastic that one wondered how it could have deceived anyone - let alone a seasoned antique dealer who ought to have smelled out a fake on sight. But then true love is blind - and notoriously silly.

The soi-disant Countess had claimed she was Anna Grimaldi, the daughter of one of the Grimaldis of Monaco (her fiction may have been inspired by the recent marriage of Grace Kelly and Prince Rainier). She said she was the widow of the Comte d'Estainville, by whom she had two children. (The d'Estainville family does exist, but this lady was not one of its members). Her family were pestering her to marry a Belgian Banker, whom she detested, so to avoid them she fled to England with her little boy. She took refuge, incognito, with a family in Peckham, and to be independent of her family she took a job as a dental nurse. Her Peckham landlady was so kind to her that she regarded her as a mother - which indeed she was. (Though, as Denys Bower told us later, she never presumed on the relationship, and when he called on the Countess she showed him respectfully to her room.)

The Countess went regularly to Chiddingstone Castle, where rooms were being prepared for her. Then, after more than a year, without any explanation she broke off the engagement. She would give Denys no sufficient explanation for the suddenness of her change of mind. Finally, in desperation, he resolved to go to her Peckham home, taking with him an antique revolver which he had had for thirty years. It had been in a job lot he had bought. The dealer had warned him that it was loaded but not knowing anything about firearms he had never tried to unload it. His plan was, if the Countess still rejected him, to take out the revolver, say that life without her was meaningless, and that he proposed to blow his brains out. The lady he thought would dissolve into tears and fall into his arms. Years later, I once asked him whether he had considered what to do if she called his bluff and said "Do as you please. Blow your brains out - it is all one to me". He said that he had not thought of that. And that, I think, was one of his failings - he had dramatic ideas, which he put into action, without thinking the consequences through - like a cat climbing to the top of a tree

5

without a thought for the descent. He had consumed a bottle of whisky the night before, while lamenting his lot, which may have given him a good deal of Dutch courage.

His plans went completely awry. When he arrived the Countess was preparing breakfast, and asked him to come back later. Why she gave him this little bit of encouragement if she never wanted to see him again, was a question never put to her.

When Denys returned she let him in but said she was going shopping. Could he not come with her, he asked. No, she said. And while she turned away to adjust the budgerigar's perch the disaster happened. Bower was taking the revolver out of his pocket when it went off accidentally. The Countess was hit. Appalled, he thought he had killed her, and without waiting to find out whether or not she was really dead, he turned the gun on himself. He succeeded in wounding himself severely and collapsed.

He came to in hospital, with a policeman standing over him. He had just enough strength to explain that Anna's father, the Count Grimaldi, must be told. The policeman greeted this request with amazement, and from this moment it seems that the police were convinced that Bower was not quite right in the head. He was left meditating on his hapless position life was even more complicated than he had thought.

Both victims had been taken to the Miller hospital in Greenwich; the Countess was released after a few days, but Bower had inflicted grave injuries on himself, which involved the removal of his spleen. This operation is now regarded as much more serious than it was then, as it can lead to serious bronchial troubles. But even in those less enlightened days, the doctors were reluctant to discharge Bower after a fortnight, but they needed the bed. He was told that he must go to another hospital for further treatment.

As he left the hospital, he was arrested, taken to court and charged with attempted murder and suicide. He was refused bail. The police said he would get just as good treatment in prison as in hospital. But when he was taken to Brixton Prison he was put in an ordinary cell and given no treatment at all. When he was brought to trial six weeks later, he was a physical wreck, in constant pain and barely able to stand or sit up.

The trial was a disgrace to British justice. The prosecution conducted their case with a vindictiveness seldom equalled, and the defence reached a similar degree of ineptitude. Bower's counsel did nothing to protect him from the bullying tactics of the prosecution. Their attitude was plain from the beginning: Bower was a rich man, who lived in a castle, terrorising a poor little girl. They alleged that he had come to Peckham planning to murder the Countess. The barrel of the gun was clean, they said, so it must have been recently loaded. (What the defence failed to point out

was that one of the features of this beautiful little weapon was that the barrel was made of a special alloy and would not be in a dirty state; and that after being loaded for so many years the slightest touch could set it off).

Even his personal achievements were derided. He had, they said done nothing with his life. (Why did the defence not point out that a year or two previously the British Museum had gratefully received a medieval Japanese lacquer casket from him?)

The Countess gave evidence for the prosecution. She was not strictly cross-examined. (Denys Bower had given instructions, though this was not made known at the trial, that nothing should be done to embarrass her. He had forgiven her the deception. He should have been warned that you cannot afford to be gentlemanly

when your freedom is at stake.)

Bower had pleaded guilty to attempted suicide, but strenuously denied the charge of attempted murder. He put up a courageous defence, although so enfeebled that at times he was barely audible.

He completely broke down when the gun was produced to him. And he was on difficult ground. His story sounded so implausible. How COULD an experienced man of the world be so taken in? The Judge's summing up was dead against him, so the jury's verdict of guilty was no surprise. The Judge postponed sentence until he had a medical report from the medical officer of Brixton Prison.

This report much impressed him and he complimented the doctor on it. He said that he appreciated that Denys Bower acted under great stress, and in addition was handicapped by bad heredity on both sides of the family. So, after due consideration, he was imposing a life sentence. In prison, he could be given suitable treatment, and could be released when the Home Office thought fit.

And now, after all these years, there he was, still in prison. We considered the jigsaw which we had put together during the last few minutes. Some pieces were missing.

Just then, afternoon tea appeared, and the guests, glad to stretch their legs, jumped up and helped each other to the delicious things. We joined in. Denys Bower went out of our minds, for the moment.

Next morning we set off for London, in the rain. It had been a miserable holiday, but for us a memorable one. It was a turning point in our lives. Never again would we be able to arrange a holiday just to suit ourselves. All the way back Ruth was haunted by the image of Denys Bower in prison - interminably. And for what? And on what evidence? Had the Judge and jury been out of their minds?

Two

The following evening, when Ruth came in from the office, she remarked that she had had a strange call from the Bank that morning. (The firm acted for the Hanover Square branch of the old Westminster Bank. Banks were not then centralised as they are now, and the major branches - and Hanover Square was the second

largest in the West End - were allowed a great deal of independence in day to day dealings, for which the Manager was responsible).

The Assistant Manager was seeking her advice about the affairs of a customer who was in very serious difficulties. He went round and round the point, Ruth said. He apologised for troubling her, said this was not the sort of thing they usually handled, would quite understand if she did not want to touch it... there was certainly no money in it... "And I wondered' she went on, 'when he was going to tell me the name of the client, for I had already guessed who it was... Denys Bower. Some intuition... I just knew".

She was quite right. Eventually the Assistant Manager brought himself to reveal the Bank's problem. They had their own worries about Bower. He explained that when Bower was buying the Castle, he had applied to the Bank for a loan, until he could make arrangements for a mortgage. He had produced for them a very convincing proposal setting out his plans for opening his house to the public. It was a time when stately homes were opening their doors - generally for tax reasons, to help with expenses. The stately owners did not propose to live on visitors' fees, as Bower hoped to do. His proposals had been well worked out, estimating expenses and returns - he had not spent the first twenty years of his working life in a bank for nothing, he knew the sort of thing that appeals to them. Banks were on the lookout for promising ventures to which they could usefully make a loan - and they lent Bower the whole of the purchase price of Chiddingstone Castle - some £6,000.

Unfortunately Bower's predictions had proved wrong. The cash flowed the wrong way out. As he said to us later, "The trouble with white elephants is that they come cheap but have voracious appetites". The Bank had never been paid a penny interest on their (temporary) loan, and now it looked as though they would lose the capital as well.

Of course, the Bank's money was in the final resort safe. It was covered twenty times by the value of the collections. But, and particularly in the present circumstances, they did not wish to do anything so drastic as selling the place up. Their many urgent letters had brought no response at all. They hardly expected to receive a reply from him, but did hope to hear from his solicitors. Denys Bower did know about their enquiries, but his solicitors had advised him not to reply, as they thought the Bank's intention was to call in the loan. This worried Bower, who knew one did not treat banks like that.

Finally Bower, frantic with worry, appealed to the Bank direct. They were touched by his letter - for Banks then had a heart, not just a computer. He was desperate about the state of affairs at the Castle. It was not being properly looked after, things were being stolen, a tenant was giving trouble. The Sunday Pictorial had written a libellous article about him, and his solicitors would not pursue the matter properly; and he was powerless to do anything about it. It was this appeal that had prompted the Assistant Manger's telephone call.

Ruth's immediate thought was: This is Destiny. I have to take it on. Since we were children, we had learned to discern the hand of Providence in our lives. Our mother was a Scot, and although not at all religious, generations of Calvinistic breeding had left its indelible mark. You accept your lot, and struggle to make the best of what has been sent you. So she asked them to send round the file, and she would look at it.

The great wadge arrived within the half hour, brought round by special messenger. On the top was Denys Bower's letter. It was written on the usual small sheet of lined paper supplied by HM prison for the use of its occupants - they were allowed two letters a month. It was headed, in DEB's bold, graceful handwriting, SOS will nobody help?

As she looked through the file, it seemed to her that his affairs were so bad that it was hopeless to try to save the Castle and its collections; perhaps, by judicious administration something might be saved out of the wreckage. She wrote to the Bank, setting out her suggestions. She had no intention of backing out of the matter. It was a case of grave injustice.

When she qualified, she had resolved not only to try to administer the law efficiently, but to see that justice was done. The two things do not necessarily coincide. But before committing herself irrevocably, she decided there were two steps she must take: see the Governor at Wormwood Scrubs, to find out more about Denys Bower - she did not want to take on a nutcase; and visit Chiddingstone Castle.

Three

The visit with the Governor was quickly arranged. She had to see the Assistant Governor who was in charge of D Wing, the part of the prison reserved for long-term offenders.

So she made her first visit to Wormwood Scrubs, which was to be a place of weekly pilgrimage for many a day. Her first impressions were even more harrowing than she had expected. The Governor's office was in a cell outside D Wing and she had just been shown in when she was told that the Governor would be delayed for some time, as some unexpected visitors had arrived who had to be dealt with immediately. So she sat and waited. From the cell door she could see the staircases and galleries of D Wing. Presently she heard a noise - voices, and banging, and clattering. It came nearer, it grew louder, the tumult became a roar such as she had never heard before. It was the prisoners being let out for their exercise period. They rushed along the galleries, hurled themselves down the stairs. The door of the 'cell' waiting room was slightly ajar and as they hurtled past she thought "they might come in and murder me, and no-one would know, there is nothing to stop them". For the first time in her life she felt really afraid; the sweat was trick ling down her back. Then the sound died away.

They came back in about a quarter of an hour, somewhat quieter. After about an hour the Governor appeared, with apologies.

Denys Bower was fortunate in one thing: his prison Governor. Jack Beaumont, assistant Governor responsible for D Block was a remarkable man and Ruth came to have a deep respect for him. Humanity, integrity of purpose, shrewdness, a sense of justice and common sense, firmness, he had all these qualities. He was besides a penetrating judge of character, and knew his prisoners as individuals.

He told Ruth that he was glad someone was at last taking an interest in Bower's case. His family never came to see him, and he had only one or two faithful friends. He himself felt deeply sorry for him, and did what he could, but he had to be careful not to show any special attention. This would soon be noticed as favouritism and would make Bower's lot even more miserable.

Ruth asked about the possibility of his release. Beaumont replied that this lay entirely in the hands of the Home Office, who were very concerned about the state of affairs at Chiddingstone Castle. Until things were put on a stable footing there, his release would not be considered. The Home Office felt that if he returned to it in its present state he would simply break down. The place must be made viable and cleared of its present habitués. He could not cope with Chidd. as it was. Also they were afraid that he might try to link up with Anna, with possible disastrous results.

"Is he dangerous?", Ruth asked.

Beaumont nearly fell off his seat laughing. "He wouldn't hurt a fly" he replied. He said that Denys had talked a lot to him about the Castle. At first, when Denys arrived at the Scrubs, weak in body and shattered in spirit, he had lost interest in life, but he now longed to be back at Chiddingstone. He was too volatile in spirits up one day and down the next. He could not escape from impotent worry about the Castle, and it was only stability there which would restore his balance.

Beaumont said that Bower came from a good background - an old well-established Derbyshire family, not aristocratic but well-established and respected. Ruth said she would think things over before deciding to take on the case. Beaumont very much hoped that she would do so - but it would be an uphill task.

Four

The next step was to visit Chiddingstone Castle. Since Bower's departure the Castle had been looked after by various friends he had made at the Royal Stuart Society, whose object is to commemorate the Royal House of Stuart. (The Society itself had nothing to do with running the place.) Denys had become interested in it because of his preoccupation with the Stuarts, and was at one time a member. Its patron was the Duchess of Alba, descendant of the Duke of Berwick and Alba, James II's distinguished natural son.

One of these friends was Major Keir, an old soldier in every sense of the word. Denys thought the world of him and when he moved to Chiddingstone Castle Major Keir moved in with him. He drank more than was good for him, which may explain his propensity for seeing ghosts. He was responsible for the legend of the Lady in Grey, who used to ride her horse up the drive. After the disaster he remained at Chiddingstone, ostensibly in charge, but whether he was altogether a loyal friend is doubtful. Sinclair (Bower's solicitor) in a letter to Keir remarked that he was inclined to agree with Keir's opinion, that Bower tended to think all his geese were swans. The implication was that the collections were worthless and therefore it did not matter how they were disposed of - and indeed quite a number of fine things just disappeared.

One morning Major Keir was found dead in bed, apparently from natural causes. He was succeeded by Hector Bruce Binney, an Old Etonian like Keir, and a member of the Royal Stuart Society. He was a connection of the Ailesburys and took the name of Bruce because he claimed to be a descendant of King Robert. He treated the Castle as his own - made alterations, as when he arranged an exhibition of avant-garde pictures, entertained lavishly at Bower's expense, ran up debts in his name, and brought friends, of whom Bower did not approve, to the place. Altogether he gave the Castle a bad name in the neighbourhood. He was once convicted of drunken driving. But Bower- as Binney knew well could not do without him.

Then an opportunity unexpectedly offered itself to get rid of Binney in the shape of a young woman who had married a member of the Royal Stuart Society. The couple had met Bower at various receptions. He had agreed to be godfather to their eldest child – no doubt he seemed a suitably affluent choice for that duty. The godmother was the Duchess of Alba, for whom the Countess stood proxy at the christening. This young lady now approached Denys very respectfully by letter. She said her marriage was breaking up, and she was looking for somewhere to live with her boyfriend and three children. She had heard that the Castle was not being well looked after by Binney. She would deem it an honour to take over as caretaker – would expect no payment - perhaps a little pocket money for the boyfriend. She would try to put things right. So Denys authorised her to become caretaker at the Castle, and left her to boot out Binney - which she did very effectively. But things at the Castle did not improve.

Ruth did not inform the 'caretaker' of her proposed visit. We just drove down to the Castle the next Saturday, like ordinary visitors. Thirty-five years ago Chiddingstone was still a completely rural corner of Kent, very hard to find, in the maze of anonymous lanes, lined with oak trees in the days of sailing ships it was reckoned that the best oak came from Chiddingstone. There was no M25 or Sevenoaks bypass. Yet, in spite of a slower car and narrow roads, it took us less time to reach Chiddingstone from central London than it does now. But even this lovely countryside looked depressing when we arrived at Chiddingstone, for it was a dull afternoon. It was April, but Spring did not seem to have arrived at the Castle. As we bumped up the drive, we could see that the waist-high grass in the North field had not been cut that season.

There was not a soul in sight as we parked our car on the apron in front of the Castle. But round the corner on the East side we found life. A young bearded man, with a small child beside him, was busy cutting turves from the lawn along the East front. He was making a very good job of it, too, and rolling them up into neat bundles. We looked at the grass; it had been good stuff once, now somewhat weedy. We passed the time of day with him; theboyfriend evidently. Then we went and rang the bell.

A swarthy young woman answered, of apparently French extraction; when inclined she could radiate charm, but this was not such an occasion. She was in a hurry, simply took our halfcrowns, sold us a little guide, and left us to find our own way about the solitude of Chiddingstone Castle.

It was the weirdest experience I have ever had. The rooms were laid out much as they are now, but that is the only resemblance to the present-day Castle. It was filthy, and it stank. I can still recall that all-pervading and idiosyncratic smell. Wet rot, dry rot, rats, mice (we saw a dead mouse on the stairs) the excreta of the two dogs who were allowed to roam the house freely and - just dirt. Denys Bower had had the whole place painted in cream emulsion, all he could afford, but that had turned to a uniform porridge colour. You might have expected to hear the ticking of the death watch beetle, but it must have been too cold for them to mate. (Actually this was the one pest from which the house was reasonably free).

The exhibits in the cases were difficult to see clearly - both they and the glass of the cases were thick with dust. We did not know anything about the Buddhistic images and Japanese works of art anyway, so our appreciation of them would have been limited even if we had seen them properly. But the manuscripts and furniture we could appreciate them and they were of fine quality.

We let ourselves out, and went silently back to the car. "Well!" said Ruth as we drove off. "I will take on the legal work but I am NOT going to look after Chiddingstone Castle".

I looked at the introduction to the little guide. It was well-written and informative. "It says", I read out, "the collections are the lifework of Denys Bower. A pity to let them go". The same thoughts were going through Ruth's mind.

Five

All this happened in the space of a few days, the matter was so urgent. The following week Ruth arranged to visit Wormwood Scrubs, with the Assistant Bank Manager, Mr. Busby, to see Denys Bower. They had to go by Underground to White City, and walk - quite a long way. On the train Mr. Busby produced, rather apologetically, two bars of KitKat. He explained that Denys Bower liked chocolate but sweets were not allowed in prison – Home Office rules. You could take a prisoner cigarettes, but not sweets, so the chocolate would have to be fed to him discreetly. Some warders were good natured and did not interfere; others pounced on the contraband. At these interviews, the prisoner was always accompanied by a warder, who sat on the other side of a glass screen, so that he could see, but not hear, all that was going on.

Denys Bower shuffled in. Ruth would not have known him, he was so changed from the debonair person he used to be. He did not recognise her and she never reminded him of their former acquaintance. Somehow it seemed tasteless to call to mind a happier past. He kept himself very neatly; his prison uniform was immaculate. This gave Ruth the wrong impression of his personal ways; she thought he must be the sort of person who keeps everything in apple pie order. Far from it. This smartness was a kind of act of defiance - prison could not grind him down, he was saying. But apart from this, he was a pathetic shadow.

They talked generally of his affairs, in particular of the libel published in the Sunday Pictorial. Ruth now got the whole story. Several weeks previously the Pictorial had published a long article, illustrated, which, among other misstatements, alleged that he was in solitary confinement in an isolated part of Parkhurst, thus implying that he was a dangerous psychopath. The article cannot have been of any real interest to their readers; Bower was not a famous (or infamous) person. The Editor must just have been short of real news, and Denys Bower's story was always good for a laugh. But the victim took the report very seriously. Looking forward to his eventual release, he feared for the effect on his reputation. However liberal-minded people may be about the mentally unbalanced, they do not readily invite them to dinner. Whereas a term in Wormwood Scrubs, the abode of normal criminals, could be lived down.

He had asked his solicitors to obtain from the Pictorial a retraction and adequate apology. These were not his original solicitors, who had acted for him at his trial. He had changed to Binney's solicitors, on the advice of his friend, but they also were proving of little help. The only acknowledgement they had received from the Sunday Pictorial was the little paragraph we had seen. Bower said that it was no apology, it was inadequate and unacceptable. But they would do no more and washed their hands of the matter.

They also discussed the financial situation. There was an urgent need of ready cash. The Bank, while generously not asking for immediate repayment of what was owed them, could hardly be expected to advance more. Could he not sell something substantial, Ruth suggested. The portrait of Nell Gwyn by Lely, for instance. No, said Bower, she is part of the

Stuart Collection. Well then, she tried again. What about the Chippendale commode in the drawing room? No, no, never that. Ruth realised that this was a cry of desperation. (She learned afterwards that this was probably his most beloved possession. His grandfather, Sam Bower, had given it to him when he was a boy - it was his first major acquisition.) She did not press the point further.

As they were leaving, Ruth looked back. Bower was hunched over the table, his head in his hands. She said: "I will try to help you." He replied, without looking up: "I do not trust any solicitor."

"Think things over, and when you wish to see me, I will come again."

That evening, Ruth told us all about the meeting. We had been all agog to hear how it had gone. And what a tragic affair it all was. It was so unjust, so unfair. I longed to do something to help.

Six

Within a couple of days Beaumont telephoned Ruth to say that Bower had asked to see her about some urgent matters. She went promptly, hoping to gain his confidence, although it disrupted her day. Nothing new had transpired since their meeting, so perhaps he did want to test her - or just longed for a chat.

At this visit she noticed one thing particularly. The light was so poor that she could not see her papers, and in the end she asked whether artificial light was not allowed. Oh yes, he said, and indicated the switch just beside her. He made no movement to turn it, and she realised how he had lost all initiative. In prison the light came on and off automatically. If there was no light you just sat. Yet he did make one effort. As Ruth stood up to go, he moved hesitantly to open the door for her. "Get back, Bower" snapped the warder. He stopped, crestfallen.

On the next visit, things began to change. Halfway through, he sat up, and his jaw seemed to snap into place. He looked more like the old Denys Bower. He must have been making his plans, for as the visit ended he sprang up so swiftly to open the door that the warder had no time to stop him. It must have been his first independent act since his imprisonment.

After that Ruth went two or even three times a week. The visits first followed a pattern. Ruth had a set of points to go through, and Bower noted them on an old envelope - all the spare paper he had, as no writing paper was allowed apart from the letter paper, which was strictly rationed per letter. After a few visits she noticed

he was no longer taking notes, and asked why. He said there was no point. She was his last line of defence. If she broke, he was finished.

These visits took a considerable amount of time, which Ruth could ill spare from a busy practice. She charged no fees for her services apart from the purely legal work on the libel action. It meant she had to make up for lost time by working in the evenings.

She saw Beaumont again after the first visit or two to Bower. He said that already there was a marked change in his outlook. He had every confidence in Ruth. Beaumont urged Ruth to take a power of attorney from him, because then she could visit as often as she liked, without getting special permission. Ruth hesitated. She told Beaumont that she was reluctant to take on the management of the Castle. He looked disappointed: the stability of the Castle was the key to Bower's release, he said. She thought of that great crumbling edifice with awe. Perhaps it was better not to think too much about it, but just take it on, and go step by step. So she took the power of attorney, and Chiddingstone Castle was in her care. She had often wondered if it would be possible to run a great mansion, and make it pay, and now she had her chance! The responsibility she had disclaimed had become hers: the care of the Castle.

On her next visit to the Castle, she introduced herself to

the 'caretaker' and told her that she was now in charge of Denys Bower's affairs, including the Castle. She looked sullen and was uncooperative, but when writing to Denys Bower she said she thought Ruth would be most helpful.

We began to visit the Castle every weekend. We watched anxiously for signs of improvement in its condition, but nothing happened. The 'caretaker' was not an efficient housekeeper. There were few visitors and we never saw tickets issued, and no accounts were kept. When Ruth asked her about this, she looked injured and said

that her boyfriend needed £10 a week - Mr. Bower had promised. That was a lot of money for us - eighty visitors at half a crown a time. I began to reckon money in terms of visitors at 2/6 - I have done so ever since and it is a salutary exercise in economy. Still, she was all we had. We could only hope for improvement.

While Ruth was engaged on other things I spent my time clearing up in the library. It had been used as a dump. Everyone who had stayed at the Castle - and there seemed to have been an odd assortment of visitors, and many of them - seemed to have abandoned their correspondence. In the first place there were the envelopes to get rid of. There were stacks and stacks of empty envelopes, but I had to look in them all to see that they really were empty. I read the correspondence and sorted it carefully. It was horrifying. The correspondents were mostly marauders of one sort or another who were gloating over the imminent break-up of the contents of the

Castle. No doubt in their minds about what Keir and Sinclair had called Denys Bower's geese "There will be some good pickings" as one of them said. Their malice towards the unfortunate Bower was beyond belief. As I sat there I could almost hear the vulture hovering over me. I felt mentally sick, and I was nearly physically sick too. It was boiling weather, and the library windows were shut fast. The all-pervading Castle stink was made worse by the fact that the Library was adjacent to the South entrance, which was the dogs' special convenience. Beaumont was right; Bower did not stand a chance amongst these hyenas. I made a packet of the particularly virulent letters, in case Denys Bower ever needed to be warned whom not to trust. And they did come in useful eventually.

Seven

As for poor Ruth where was she to begin? The immediate danger was that there were writs out against Bower, for debts incurred in his name by Binney. The services were on the point of suing. The grounds had to be got into some sort of order to attract visitors - though it did have a lure for some as the Castle of Horrors, and our first improvements disappointed these patrons and were too slight to attract others. There was no capital - none. And there were also the 'trespassers' in the Castle.

One of these was a school teacher who was occupying the flat now known as 2 Castle Close. His tenancy was quite unauthorised, probably let in by Binney. When Ruth delivered the ultimatum, he replied with a long harangue, and ended with the hope that Ruth's ego was satisfied now that she was turning everyone out of the

Castle. Nevertheless, he went.

The other 'trespasser' came as a surprise to her. One day, when walking round the Castle when it was closed, she came across a complete stranger. He turned out to be a former friend of Bower. In return for a loan he was allowed to occupy certain rooms at the Castle. The loan was repaid - Denys happened to have some ready money from his mother's estate - but the 'friend' did not depart. His apartments communicated with the Castle and that was how he happened to meet Ruth. So he had to be told firmly that his connection with the Castle was ended. The vacating of these two sets of rooms - they could hardly be called flats - assisted Ruth with an idea she was evolving: if they could be converted into real letting flats (with the aid of a loan from the Bank!) they could provide a steady income for the Castle. A flat was already let in the coach-house, and the tenant fortunately paid regularly.

Ruth dealt with the creditors by writing to each individually, explaining that she had taken over the management, that she was sure finances could be put on a satisfactory footing, would pay them by instalment and give them a two-monthly report. They all co-operated, and some were very sporting. The Post Office reduced the telephone bill - a number of unauthorised calls had been made to the U.S.A. The oil suppliers for the central heating said they had given up hope of being paid and had written off the account as a bad debt. So they offered renewal of the contract on

extremely generous terms.

Ruth went ahead very quickly with her plans for the flats. When she had agreed to take over the running of the Castle, she had pointed out to the Bank that it was essential to have a source of regular income, and so she asked them to make a loan for the conversion of the two flats. They had given her a difficult - some would say impossible - task - she had got them out of a difficult situation – and they followed her advice on how to accomplish it. They agreed to lend £4,000-5,000 - a very reasonable amount. But first, they said they would like to have an assessment of the viability of the project from a reputable London Estate Agent. So they arranged for someone to come down from London.

When he arrived he was told to go across the courtyard, where he would find the 'flats'. The dogs were loose in the courtyard. They were fierce animals and he, wisely, did not attempt the journey but took a distant look at the flats. That was enough. He took a very poor view of their potential attractions.

Nonetheless, the plan went on. Ruth had been recommended to consult a distinguished Tunbridge Wells architect, Mr. Cecil Burn of Cecil Burns & Guthrie. He was then at the end of a long career.

He had a deep knowledge of the problems of old buildings and was one of the few architects left with a sound grasp of Classical principles. One of his works is the Neo- Queen Anne post office at the right-hand side (ascending) of the London Road. I hope it is listed. It deserves to be. His wife came along to the first meeting – a charming woman, she brought a picnic and we all joined in.

Eight

Mr. Burns fell head over heels in love with the Castle, at first sight. This was heartening, because the architectural establishment regarded the Castle Style with contempt - indeed hardly architecture at all. He urged Ruth to consider the possibility of converting the second floor of the North Front to flats, including some of the first floor. Ruth pointed out that an insuperable difficulty was that most of the second floor windows began at floor level and ended at waist height, to preserve the external proportions of the facade. Besides there were security and safety risks, especially fire. She could have hardly spoken more strongly. The project would need planning permission, a complication she wished to avoid. The existing flats were merely being refurbished. Nevertheless within a few days she received plans for the North Wing alterations. She returned them without even looking at them afterwards - we regretted this, because we would have liked to know how he dealt with those windows.

Her only comment was to say that on no account to put in these proposals for planning permission. Too late. He had already done so.

Almost immediately the Fire Officer descended on the

Castle. He could hardly find words to express his (quite justifiable) horror. He said that floors, ceilings, walls, the Great Staircase, would have to be lined with asbestos. Burns thought the Fire Officer took an exaggerated view of the risk, but his opposition put an end to the North Wing project without any argument. Many years later, when official views on asbestos had changed, Ruth wondered what would have happened if we had carried out the Fire Officer's requirements.

An unfortunate result of the North Wing project was that the rumour went round the village that the Castle was to be converted into flats, and this aroused much hostility. Relations with the Castle were strained anyway - this only made things worse.

Nine

While this was going on at the Castle Ruth was working on another matter - arranging with the Home Office for Denys Bower to visit Chiddingstone. This was not a happy frolic, it had a serious purpose. Bower suspected that things were being stolen, and only he could tell what was missing. The contents had not been properly catalogued and there were few photographs. From time to time the Evening Standard used to have little snippets about how Denys Bower was allowed to visit the Castle at weekends, but in fact such leniency was not in the mind of the Home Office. Ruth had to put the case in the most urgent terms before they reluctantly agreed to let him have a day's leave. I typed all the correspondence - fortunately at one time I had learned to type, and with all this practice became quite good at it. It was the only way to make sure of complete confidentiality - and this was hot stuff - and besides we could not afford a professional typist. When I thought Ruth's language was not strong enough I asked if I could pep it up. She sometimes gave me a little licence, but said it would do no good. It did not - the Home Office was quite unmoved, but it relieved my feelings.

At length everything was arranged. The visit was handled very discreetly at Wormwood Scrubs, so that the press should have no inkling of what was going on. A prison officer would accompany Denys Bower, and Ruth would call for them by car at the prison. She had informed them at the Castle, enjoining them to complete

secrecy, and asking to have lunch prepared.

Early in the morning of the visit Beaumont telephoned Ruth. The visit was off - cancelled. The press had got wind of it. One or two reporters had telephoned that morning to ask if the information were true. It seemed that the press was preparing a royal reception at Chiddingstone. If they had got so much out of imaginary visits, what would they not have made of a real one? It is sad that the popular press waste so much time and money out of purveying silly gossip, when there are much graver matters to be brought to public notice - and matters which could be presented in an interesting way too. The Great Public has quite a lot of good sense, however low the popular press may rate it. And it was not really interested in Denys Bower; no-one bothered to raise any query when one paper announced he was confined in Parkhurst, and another that he was allowed to spend weekends at Chiddingstone Castle.

On this occasion they got no story, for Ruth drove down to the Castle alone. The caretaker appeared smiling at the door. Ruth announced the non-arrival of Denys Bower, on account of the Press's knowledge of his intended visit. "You told them"

Ruth said. The caretaker admitted that she had - she thought it would do no harm. Ruth reminded her that she had been sworn to absolute secrecy. They parted without further comment, but Ruth knew that she had another eviction problem on her hands.

Another visit was shortly arranged. This time Ruth told

no-one. She just took a picnic - and it was a lovely picnic too. Ruth asked Denys Bower what he would prefer, and he chose steak and kidney pie. So my mother, who made the most delicious pies I have ever tasted, made one specially. The prison officer who accompanied Bower had been specially chosen by Beaumont. The calibre of the officers varied greatly. Some, Bower said, were sheer sadists. Others regarded their work more as a social service, and took their obligations very seriously. This seemed to be so especially in the case of officers where prison service was a family tradition. Such was Anning, the 'duenna' on this occasion. He behaved with great tact, joined in the picnic and cleared up afterwards. Bower was so excited that he could not eat anything, but Ruth was glad she had something nice for Anning, who enjoyed it.

Denys Bower's visit was of course quite unexpected at the Castle. No sign of the press this time. It was a busy day - the main object was to check what was missing. There had been some dissension over ownership with Binney, who claimed that the Japanese lacquer writing box from the famous Seymour Trower Collection was his. He had taken it with him, and Ruth was taking proceedings against him for its return. But another loss which Denys had not suspected, had occurred. As soon as he entered the Egyptian Rooms he exclaimed "Where's Mahu?", and went towards a case where there was a kneeling figure. It had been substituted for Mahu. Mahu was also a kneeling figure, but more imposing, of a priest. It was the most valuable object in the whole collection. Binney had assured him it was safe.

The substitution must have taken place before our advent, for we had not seen Mahu. He was a distinctive figure, and even to non-Egyptologists like ourselves the change would have been obvious. The police made some tentative enquiries, Ruth did what she could, but Mahu was never found and has never been heard of since.

This incident showed the strong side of Bower's character. He had been dealt a shattering blow, but he did not brood over it. He was remarkably free of self-pity. He put disaster behind him. What had happened, he said, was past and irrevocable. You must always look to the future. It was this streak of toughness that had saved him in prison.

Ten

The final episode in the caretaker's career at the Castle came a week or two later, with the Grand Party. One Saturday Ruth and I arrived at the Castle to find lively preparations going on. The White Rose Drawing Room was laid out with decorations and candles - all amidst the dust and squalor, it could have been a filmset for Miss Havisham's wedding celebrations. Evidently it was to be quite an event.

Ruth said that on no account was the White Rose Drawing Room to be used for such a purpose. She pointed out that frightful damage might be done to the works of art there. The candles might set the place on fire and the whole Castle might be burned down.

Ruth spoke in the strongest possible terms and said that if she persisted in holding the party Mr. Bower would be informed of her complete unworthiness for her position.

We left, feeling very worried and utterly despondent. When we returned next day our worst fears were not justified, for the Castle was still there, intact. But the Drawing Room was spattered everywhere with candle grease - the candles had simply overflowed from the great ormolu candlesticks. The party had gone on into the early hours. Several of the guests had ended the celebrations by a dip in the swimming pool of our neighbour Colonel Cox (he had the gardener's house and kitchen garden which had formerly belonged to the Castle).

We drove back to London in a state of despair and utter resignation. Despair - how to deal with the security of the Castle. Ruth had hoped, when she took it on, that at least there was a responsible person living there; but what now? Resignation - because we knew there was no turning back from our destiny.

Ruth's first anxiety was: how would Denys Bower take disappointment over the caretaker's capabilities? To Ruth's relief, he was quite firm, fully agreed that she must go and signed her letter of dismissal, leaving to Ruth the task of evicting her.

The problem was really resolved by the caretaker herself. She made a fundamental tactical error. She moved from Denys Bower's quarters in the Castle to the flat recently vacated. Ruth found her there, gave her the letter of dismissal, and pointed out that the builders were expected at any moment to begin work on the

refurbishment. She left without more ado, with her boyfriend and children.

A brief inspection of Denys Bower's flat revealed chaos. It was dirty and dusty as the rest of the Castle. The yellow Satin Regency curtains were quite grey, torn to ribbons in places. There was an unemptied child's potty under the kitchen sink, and - very peculiar - there were a lot of pheasant's feathers floating around. We had to

leave it for the time being; it would be hard work to make it fit for its owner again.

So we left that great house, completely empty of life, unsecured, without any protection. The great Drawing Room had not even any shutters. There was nothing so sophisticated as a burglar alarm. Yet no-one troubled to break in. No-one, of course thought there was anything of value in the Castle. But nowadays vandals would come in and smash up a house like that, just for the fun of it.

The precincts, however, were not quite deserted. There was a tenant in the 'cottage' which had been carved out of the coach house; and there was Mankelow, the handyman and gardener who was a legacy from the school, the previous owner of the castle.

Mankelow is an ancient Kentish name, and the man himself we felt, was of Kentish origin. His ancestors had probably lived in the great forests of the Weald, spare, wiry, and immensely strong, before the Norman Conquest, charcoal burners or swineherds. Once, we were going round the grounds, considering the problem of getting up some saplings. He simply took hold of one, twisted. and turned it, and up it came by the roots. "Easy," he said. But he never did it again. The saplings grew up into a birch wood and are there to this day.

We could never think of Mankelow as quite real- he was something out of a folk tale - and we were surprised one day when he said he was going to visit his sister. He did not live in the castle itself, but in a room in the connecting corridor between the main house and the coach house. It had been part of the butler's offices. He looked after himself. He was no cook, and once, greatly daring, he bought a tinned pudding from the village shop. But he put it straight on to the electric stove, without reading the instructions. It exploded, and the contents went all over the room, to his indignation.

One of his duties was to go round the attics and to keep emptied the large basins that were placed strategically to catch the rain which poured through the leaking roofs. When he heard that Ruth was hoping to get the roofs repaired he expressed his disapproval. Waste of money. The roof had leaked ever since he had known it and always would. Easier to keep the basins. (It must be admitted that Mankelow was right. Nearly half a million has been spent on the roofs. They still leak, and we still have to rely on basins.)

As an employee, Mankelow had two outstanding advantages. He did not mind what he did. His first job with us was to clean out the south entrance which was thick with dog faeces. It was a foul task, and he did it thoroughly and uncomplainingly without any new-fangled modern equipment. He was also completely honest, so far as money was concerned. Still, we never felt at ease with him. Neither did Denys, who said he tried to avoid him whenever possible. Mankelow, for his part, had already told us, "Mr Bower is sennetric, very sennetric. He'll be coming towards you and then suddenly run and go in the opposite direction."

Eleven

Ruth now faced with resignation the depressing truth. She would obliged to run Chiddingstone Castle on her own. In a way it was an exciting prospect. Adventures like this do not happen very often in one's life. It had a peculiar quality. It was not like a personal problem which affects one's internal life and one's whole future. It preoccupied our minds; we cared about it intensely. But if Chiddingstone foundered we should go on just as we had previously, very much sadder, but materially undamaged.

And how would it go on? How much time must we devote to it? The answer to the first question lay entirely in the hands of the Home Office, but surely they could not delay Deny' release much beyond five years - this was reckoned to be the minimum for a life sentence. As for the second question - the answer was quite clear: all our spare time and for Ruth, it meant a good deal of her business as well. She was busy enough already: the time necessary for the prison visits was just about the last straw. Yet she never once considered withdrawing from what she considered her destiny.

Our parents very gallantly offered to do all they could to help. We went to the Castle every Saturday and Sunday, driving down from town each day. The journey took 1 hour 25 minutes - less if we were lucky. (The same journey, with a faster car and the improvements on the A21, now takes 1 and 3/4 hours.) For the rest of that

Summer 1961 it was just a question of keeping going as best we could, and make plans for what we would do in the Winter.

During the week - the Castle was open every day except Monday - Mankelow let in the visitors. They made their own way around the Castle. There was not much loose property they could take. Fortunately no-one tried to smash open the cases - things were not so lawless then as they are now. It was in the grounds that we had

most trouble. A lot of the visitors were very rough types, who picknicked and sunbathed where they liked, and they really had to be booted out. The Castle was well-known, apparently, for being a free-for-all place. At weekends our parents helped with visitors. My mother did some very hard work, cleaning and polishing the cases and furniture.

We had a lightning programme. As soon as we arrived, we dashed into the Castle to do what tidying we could. Denys Bower's apartments needed emergency attention. Mankelow did the worst of the cleaning, but we had to deal with the ever present pheasant feathers. When we came to look closely, there were great stacks of feathers under the beds, in cupboards, up chimneys ... Someone had been living well. We bundled them up discreetly in plastic bags. Then there were the attics. One room was filled with flies. They buzzed round and round - it was impossible to go into the room. So we bought some lethal fly killer, and next weekend we entered the

weekend after, hardly a fly was surviving, and we swept up the room, masked and hooded, and sprayed in all directions. The corpses with great satisfaction. We repeated the treatment every week.

Afterwards we went into the grounds and frantically tried

to clear the flower beds around the Castle and in the courtyard garden. We knew nothing about gardening; if we had I don't think we would have tackled the job. We bought a wonderful implement (for there were no garden tools) - a Wolf Hoe. Ruthlessly handled, this commits mayhem. It used to come up festooned with weeds. I joined the RHS and the National Rose Society, and made plans for the following spring.

One afternoon when we were working up by the Orangery - a ruin, alas - we came across a stranger, very reputable, not one of our usual gate crashers, but an amiable countryman in tweeds. We enquired who he was, letting him know who we were. He told us he was one of Lord Astor's keepers. Lord Astor had the shooting rights over the grounds, and the keeper was making his usual inspection. Lord Astor still preserved, and the keeper said they were a bit worried about poachers - they had lost a lot of pheasants recently. We felt embarrassed - we could tell him where some of his pheasants had gone – but we felt we did not know him well enough to say that his troubles were over. We told him instead that we were trying to pull the place up. He smiled sympathetically, and remarked that we had a hard task ahead.

We guessed that he felt sorry for us, but he and his family were to show more than just sympathy. He was Mr Veall, and his wife and two boys were to give immense help.

By this time Chiddingstone was becoming an addiction. We begrudged every moment we spent away from it. We had always been interested in country houses. When we had been members of the Georgian Group we had had the opportunity of seeing many lovely houses still in private occupation. So although we had never lived in a great house ourselves, we knew what it should look like and feel like. Each country house has its own atmosphere – the poor forlorn Castle had lost its soul – we must help to find it.

Twelve

Another of Ruth's earliest preoccupations was finding means of paying off the Castle debts. There was no ready money of course, but there were still some quite valuable items which could be realised. They were not part of the collections and Denys was quite willing that they should be sold. It was we in fact who were sorrier to see them go, we liked them so much.

There were three items of silver: a small exquisite George II salver, a George III water jug; and a magnificent Baroque George II coffee pot. All these were put up for auction at Sotheby's, Denys fixing the reserves. This is extremely important when selling at an auction. The auctioneer's judgement is not always reliable.

The sale of the water jug did not prove straightforward. When we went to view we saw it had been bashed. We reproached Sotheby's for careless handling. They were rather stand-offish at first, but when they realised how entirely innocent we were, they explained. They had recently had a spate of silver bashing. Viewers were

allowed a fair amount of freedom in examining objects, and some unscrupulous dealers were suspected of damaging silver to put off the amateur buyer, who does not like having to get things repaired. The amateur (as distinct from the serious collector) was just beginning to frequent the auction rooms. They were disliked by dealers for they put up prices; they were often one-off buyers who were prepared to pay over the top for their heart's desire - and they were the enemy of the ring. Sothebys had the jug repaired and it sold satisfactorily.

The little salver did not reach its reserve at the first sale. When Ruth went down to Sotheby's to enquire about its fate, and heard, she involuntarily gave a despairing cry and said, "but I must have the money!" The assistant dashed off to fetch Mr Rose, the Head of the Silver Department. He explained gently that Sotheby's did not buy things, but only offered them for sale. If there were no takers the goods did not sell. Ruth explained that she knew this very well. She had not been able to help giving an exclamation of disappointment, and she told him why, and who was really the seller. Mr Rose was most sympathetic, He remembered Bower well, said he was not at all like other antique dealers in his ways, and added, "He was absolutely straight, you could trust him absolutely." The salver eventually went for thirty pounds.

The coffee pot would, we hoped, fetch £200, but auctions are, even with the most desirable objects, somewhat of a gamble. To make sure it fetched what it ought, I volunteered to go to the sale, to bid it up if necessary - a practice which was frowned on then and is forbidden now. It could be very effective if bidding sagged or if a ring

were in operation. My place of work was just on the other side of Green Park, the coffee pot was due to come about lunchtime, so I could easily run across to the sale in my lunch hour. (Bidding at auction was not unusual for me. I collected in a very modest way - English porcelain, mostly cracked, for that was cheaper and it was the only way I could afford good examples.) But no amount of bidding had taught me to control my excitement this time. It quite took it out of me.

This experience was even more exciting than usual, for it was really important.

I arrived at the sale room in good time. The coffee pot came up. Bidding stopped at around £120; I nudged it up. It reached £160. I bid again - and was left with it at £165. The next day *The Times* sales report (they published them daily then) announced that Mrs Eldridge had acquired a Georgian coffee pot for £165. Whether I

was awarded this distinction because the reporter thought this was a noteworthy bargain we could not decide. More likely he thought I had paid through the nose.

We never again tried to sell that coffee pot. When Denys Bower had the money he bought it back from us. It stood on his sideboard until he died. It was a gorgeous thing - when my mother polished it. He always used it - with Woolworth's powdered coffee. It deserved Nestles best but he never rose to that.

The other main items were books. At the time books were difficult to sell profitably, Most of the buyers were dealers. - very little arnateur competition, except perhaps for a very unusual item. But Denys had at least kept up with current prices through the catalogues they sent to him, and he instructed Ruth what yalue should be put on each item. Sotheby's wanted t to sell the books in one lot, saying they were not worth selling individually. Denys countered by pointing out that all the items had recently been sold individually, giving chapter and verse. Ruth had to pass on all the messages - with adequate forcefulness. It all took up time but was most instructive. In the end I think we must both have been amongst the most accomplished amateur sellers at auctions.

There were two books we really regretted - two folio volumes of Sheraton's furniture design which Denys had himself bound in full leather. They were beautifully done. But to buy them ourselves would have been foolish, even by our standards. They would command a good price; and for general use, reproductions (which we

had) were just as effective. So we let them go.

Ruth succeeded in paying off the debts, The Castle has never owed money since. The debt she most begrudged paying, was £1200 owed to Sinclair, Bower's first solicitor. It was an extortionate charge for ineffectual work but there was little to be done as Wainwright, the next solicitor, had agreed it. There was one item however which Ruth got removed. Sinclair had charged fees for attending auction sales of items from the collections. This was quite unnecessary anyway, as Sinclair (by his admission) knew nothing about works of art. The bill was finally agreed at £800 - worth it, for it proved to be the price of Bower's release.

The bill was to be paid off over four years, but Sinclair at once handed over all the papers relating to Bower and his trial. Amongst these was a very interesting document - a carbon copy of the report of the medical examination on Denys Bower - the report I have previously mentioned. An essential aspect of the report was its insistence on the (supposed) fact that Bower came from poor stock, hence his extraordinary behaviour over Anna. This report would be passed to counsel for the defence before sentence was passed, but he had let it pass without comment. Neither had Sinclair mentioned it to Ruth - perhaps he thought it was fair comment, simply confirming his own opinion of Bower.

Thirteen

Ruth was now to find out what 'poor stock' meant. The contents of the report were a worthy continuation of the Gilbert and Sullivan atmosphere of the trial, and briefly, it was based on the following premises:-

1. Bower's mother had a stepsister who had been confined in her old age in a mental asylum, where she died. Another stepsister also stayed in the asylum as a voluntary patient.
2. A stepbrother of his mother had committed suicide.
3. His mother was of a hysterical and unstable disposition.
4. On his father's side, a great grandfather had had a mental breakdown.

A step relation is no blood relation , a fact known to every child familiar with the story of Cinderella. But apparently it was a little point which escaped the notice of the judge, the Permanent Under Secretary at the Home Office, and the Home Secretary himself, R. A. Butler.

At their next meeting, Ruth asked Bower if he knew about the report. He said he had been given it to read after he had been in prison for some time. Concerned at the aspersions cast on his family, he had complained to Beaumont so persistently that the Home Office had agreed he could see the report, but that he could not have a copy. But he had an excellent memory, and he could repeat it almost verbatim. He told Ruth of the circumstances in which it had been made.

He was of course in a state of great weakness and agonising pain when it had been made but his mind was quite clear. Dr Matheson asked whether there was any history of mental instability in his family. When he replied that there was none - on the contrary his relations were all very well-balanced - Dr Matheson asked him to think again very carefully. It was in his interest to produce some evidence of mental trouble as this could ameliorate the sentence. So Bower thought desperately, bat this was all he could come up with.

His maternal grandmother had married twice. By her first marriage she had had a son and two daughters. The son had committed suicide when Denys Bower was a child - he had never been told why. The two daughters lived to a good age, but one became senile (Alzheimer's disease) and had to go into the local mental asylum as a voluntary inmate – there was nothing wrong with her mentally but she could not live alone.

The grandmother married a second time, and amongst her children was Bower's mother and a son Leo who became quite a well-known artist. Dr Matheson's terminology was confused. Denys Bower was sure he had said 'half' not 'step' but the report was never read back to him at that time, so he could not make any corrections. Perhaps Dr Matheson did not know the difference. However that may be, he had made an appalling blunder. A 'step' is no blood relation, and it is extremely difficult, and dangerous to make deductions where half-blood is concerned.

As for Denys' mother, she was an exceedingly rational woman, but she had an unusually bad time at the menopause. From being known for hospitality - apparently famed for her tea parties, they were mentioned in her obituary in the local paper - she became reclusive, but she recovered and died at the age of seventy-six.

On his father's side, a great grandfather had had a nervous breakdown in middle age. Bower would not have known about this if his mother had not mentioned it at one time. Great grandfather had owned some kind of textile mill. In the 1860's new machinery had been invented which he failed to introduce, believing it to be a passing phase. He was wrong, and in consequence went out of business. The strain brought on a nervous breakdown, but in six months he had recovered. He started again, and this time all went well.

Out of this flimsy evidence Dr Matheson had fabricated a pseudo-scientific report – perhaps he really believed it. Perhaps he thought he was helping Denys by his fairy tale, and was taken aback at the severity of the sentence. As soon as Denys had read the report he complained to the Home Office, pointing out the truth, but they took no notice. Perhaps they thought it was safer to keep him inside. If he was released, the popular Press would be waiting at the gates of Wormwood Scrubs for his story. If he remained in prison, he would eventually in the nature of things expire quietly and that would save the Home Office a lot of worry, and no questions asked. One can see their predicament.

Ruth realised she had an invaluable weapon, and pondered on her next step. Beaumont had told her that a review of Bower's case was due in November, and the prison authorities would report favourably and advise his release. If the Home Office were going to agree to release him anyway, it might be best to lie low for the time being - any interference might only annoy them and delay matters.

Besides, here was the possibility of help from elsewhere. Christmas Humphreys - at that time a Recorder - was a friend of Bower. He said he knew the judge and would speak to him about the sentence. (Nothing ever came of this). Humphreys and Bower were fellow Buddhists - the former a serious one, Bower just a romantic, attracted by the beautiful imagery of Buddhism, of which he possessed a good quantity, and by the pacific nature of its credo. He told Ruth wryly it did no good at his trial. For before the verdict his Counsel jumped up and said he had just learned that his client was a Buddhist, and therefore that the peaceful nature of his beliefs would preclude any murderous intentions. Bower said that he realised that so far as the judge and jury were concerned, that was the last straw.

Sinclair's papers revealed one or two other interesting things. After the trial he was approached by the British Museum, enquiring what was to happen to the collections, because there were certain things they wished to buy. Sinclair ignored their request, but instead allowed a local antique dealer, the Obelisk Gallery, to take its pick. They chose the objects designated by the British Museum, and sold them on to the Museum at a considerable profit. When Ruth reproached Sinclair with this, he said he had supposed the BM wanted them as a gift. Denys Bower may well have been a difficult client, but he certainly had good grounds for complaining about his solicitor.

Fourteen

Every Saturday and Sunday we went down to the Castle. There was so much to do there that we had no time to think what a fantastic undertaking its rehabilitation would be. Even in its dilapidated state it looked lovely in the Autumn sunlight; we used to think of its owner, in prison, unable to enjoy it – would he ever return as a free man?

We were desperate to find a couple to act as custodians, and our advertisement in *The Lady* certainly brought a massive response – under a box number of course. Most of the applicants were quite unsuitable, their only qualification being that they desperately needed accommodation. Some of the cases were pathetic indeed. But there was one outstanding couple, and one was all we needed.

Mr Waters was appropriately enough a water engineer, just retired. He and his wife had planned to join up with her sister and brother-in-law and go to live in the West Country in adjacent cottages. At the last moment the brother-in-law decided to postpone his plans. The Waters were left stranded, having given up their flat, and at a loose end for two years.

They were amongst the best custodians we have ever had, and without them we could not have managed at this dangerous juncture. Mr Waters was intelligent, practical, used to responsibility, and of distinguished appearance; qualities which were to stand us in good stead during the troubled months ahead, when several times he had to deal with an obtrusive press.

Mrs Waters was kindly, conscientious and hospitable. Whenever we arrived at the weekend, there she was welcoming us with coffee and cakes. We quite enjoyed our visits, hard work though they were. Mrs Waters was also kind to Mankelow, providing him with titbits; which was all the kinder because she disliked him really. He remained at the Castle until just before DEB's return, then suddenly he told the Waters he was going, and just went – disappeared.

Our evenings were often devoted to Chiddingstone too. We were going to upholstery classes. They were held at the old Regent Street Polytechnic, and our instructor was Heal's soft furnishings estimator, who at that time was dealing with the refurbishment of Buckingham Palace. So we were trained on the best principles, even if we could not always observe them. We decided to employ our time doing up Chiddingstone. We re-hung a large four-poster bed; made new loose covers for the arm-chairs, and unlimited sets of curtains. As we had so little money we bought what job lots of materials we could find. Our piece de resistance was the yellow satin Regency curtains in the sitting room. They were grey with dirt, badly split, even hanging in ribbons.

When we dismantled them we found a child's toy in the interlining. We were inspired by our memory of Lady Meade-Featheringstonehaugh at Uppark, restoring the eighteenth century curtains. She had washed them in sarponaria officinalis, stretched them on a frame and stitched down the fragmented material – Loves Labour Lost, for all the work was destroyed in the great fire at Uppark. We tacked the dirty satin curtains onto a muslin, washed the soiled bits carefully, and finally let into the rinsing bath a large unsullied turning of the material. The yellow dye floated out and brought the whole curtain back – more or less – to its original bright colour. Then we interlined and relined them. We did the same with some pale green silk brocaded Victorian curtains, but some builders who came in after Denys Bower's death used them as floor cloths, and that was the end of them. Life at Chiddingstone can be discouraging!

I don't think Denys Bower appreciated all these details when he came back. He had rather the insouciance of a child, a nice child, who expects those whom he trusts to be nice to him, and would be rather hurt and bewildered if they were not.

We were devoting so much of our time to Chiddingstone that some of our friends were becoming rather cross with us. We had had a very busy social life – out almost every evening. Now the Castle had become our VOCATION. But just for a limited time. One day we would hand it back to its owner, and in the meantime we must do all we could to get it into some sort of shape.

Fifteen

By this time Bower was in a buoyant mood. The change in his fortunes since Ruth had taken over his affairs was indeed incredible. He felt certain that he would be released at the next review, though Beaumont was not so sanguine. He remarked to Ruth that Bower still had his bad days. He was temperamentally unstable, and it was essential to keep him on a level course. So Ruth did all she could to make him feel part of Chiddingstone again. She told him all that was going on. No decision was taken without his approval. When we bought materials, he was shown the pattern first. He seemed quite impressed with our taste. On every visit she took him truffles – Charbonnel & Walker truffles. The little balls could easily be rolled to him under cover of a document.

Some emotional crises had they occurred would not have been surprising in his circumstances. What was remarkable was his lack of self-pity, and the philosophical resignation with which he accepted his fate. He was struggling against it, but he did not moan, and he was always looking to the future. Now at last, he saw the real prospect of a future.

He could take a detached view of his surroundings. He told Ruth that from his cell window he could just see part of a tower of Wormwood Scrubs. "Quite Chinese," he said. The architecture of the place had some good points, he thought. He had his cell to himself, though so filled with books and pamphlets he could hardly move; and solitude did not worry him. He had quite a lot of time to himself because he had been excused from the 'association', and when he was better he asked Beaumont If he could be released from this pleasure on health grounds. He did not relish the idea of mixing with other prisoners, and he thought they might take an unhealthy interest in his collections. Beaumont granted his request. You had to be careful, Bower explained to Ruth, not to seem stand-offish; otherwise you might meet with unexplained accidents, like falling downstairs.

He made the best of his confinement by learning a new craft – book-binding. For some reason the Home Office had decided that book-binding would be a therapeutic occupation for prisoners, and had appointed a skilled book-binder as instructor.

Rather a strange choice of craft, one would think, for book-binding calls for the use of razor-sharp tools. In spite of that attraction it does not seem to have been wildly popular. Perhaps Beaumont vetted the pupils. So it must have been an unexpected pleasure to the instructor to have a pupil who was a distinguished bibliophile and connoisseur of great binding. Bower made remarkable progress – even though his right hand was disabled. As a young man he had been knocked off his motor cycle by a lorry which had driven over his right hand. At first it was thought he would lose the crushed hand, but it recovered some movement. He could grip a pen between thumb and first finger, and learnt to write again – a most beautiful elegant hand. But that was all the hand could do.

So he spent all his 'association' time binding. Most of the work he did was on small books – the rebinding of his Jacobite pamphlets. He had one of the finest collections in the country. Pamphlets were a popular means in the eighteenth century of distributing personal views on politics, religion – anything. When the contemporary collector had bought a few he had them bound up together for his library. Usually about half a dozen would make one sizable book. So you would get all sorts of subjects under one binding. Denys split up these books to take out the Jacobite pamphlets and bind them separately. It may seem vandalism to treat an eighteenth century binding so cavalierly, but in many cases the leather would be perishing anyway and the routine library binding was not particularly distinguished.

Whist Denys was developing a new skill, other prisoners were trying to keep up their old professional skills. They were allowed to watch television and to choose their programme. They always chose a crime film – a whodunnit. They would watch very attentively and afterwards hold an inquest on the film. Why had the plan failed? (And of course it always did – though the police are rarely so successful in real life.) Was there any way in which it could have been improved? Did it give any hints of practical use at some future happy date?

All the prisoners in D Block were on long term sentences. The young ones, on remand, were confined separately; perhaps the Home Office thought they would be contaminated by the old lags. But Beaumont once remarked to Ruth that these young offenders were the ones which made him apprehensive. He was right. We are now seeing the activities of these young wrong doers in their maturity – and the legacy they have bestowed on their children.

Sixteen

At the visits, a perpetual subject for discussion was the libel action against the *Sunday Pictoral*. Ruth was pursuing this vigorously. She had consulted Granville Wingate, who had not then taken silk. As a leader, Bower wished to take in Helenus Milmo, who had recently had resounding success in libel actions. It was a good choice, but there was the question of Milmo's fees – they would be extremely high. Bower was quite certain he would win his case – clients usually are – but a good lawyer knows that the results of litigation are uncertain, and a good settlement out of court is preferable. That was not possible in this case. The *Sunday Pictoral* was belligerent and contemptuous. They took the view that a criminal serving a life sentence had lost all claim to a reputation. What claim had he to a good name, who had already lost everything? A jury might well think along the same lines. Besides, there was the inherent danger that the defendant might pay damages into court before the case came on, based on what he thought the Court might award. If the plaintiff went ahead nevertheless, and the Court awarded the same or less damages, he would have to pay the costs of both sides, incurred after the date of the payment into court.

Eventually Bower agreed that if the ultimate disaster occurred he would sell the Egyptian collections to pay the costs of the action.

It was esstential therefore, if Bower was to have a good chance of winning the action, that the Home Office should have agreed to his release. This called for a timetable. The action, if things proceeded normally, would be due to come on the following June; so it would be necessary to have the Home Office give their decision before this date. The result of the regular review would probably not be known until Christmas or thereabouts. If adverse, that left five months to get it reversed. A tight schedule. Ruth, who never left anything to chance made her contingency plans.

She made an analysis of Dr Matheson's report, relating his conclusions first to the facts as he supposed them to be, and then to the facts as they were. His errors were exposed conclusively. But these were only her views and though some of them hardly needed medical support she knew she must obtain strong expert backing, which there might be professional reluctance to give. But she had recently met Dr Laing, the distinguished psychiatrist, and when she put the case to him he responded immediately. He said he would be happy to give all the help he could (he had no fear of authority), the report was absolute nonsense – in particular Dr Matheson's views on hysteria which was one of Dr Laing's specialisms.

The next problem would be to get the report direct to the Home Secretary, R A Butler. There was no use sending it through the routine Home Office channels. It would simply end with the permanent Under Secretary; or might not even reach him. It must be submitted to someone who would give it to Butler and make sure he read it. And who better than the Lord Chancellor, the Head of the legal profession.

At that time the Lord Chancellor was Lord Kilmuir whom Ruth knew personally. She was a friend of the family.

She knew him to be a very fair and humane man, and when Ruth had qualified as a solicitor he had told her that if ever he could give her any help in her profession, he would willingly do so. It was an invaluable offer to a young solicitor, but she had never taken advantage of it. Now however, she might take it up – not for herself, but for someone else's need. But she held back that final act until she had the result of the sentence review.

Seventeen

As Ruth held a power of attorney from Bower, her visits did not come from his official ration. (That power was never revoked). He had few friends however, to take it up. His family never visited him. But he had one good friend, CAOLONEL ion Munro, a Scot and fellow Jacobite. He had had a distinguished career as a journalist. He had been the *Morning Post* correspondent in Italy, and was fluent in several languages. He told Ruth that he had met the Countess, and when he was introduced he began talking to her in French. She replied in English saying coyly that she liked to take every opportunity of talking English. He said she was a demure young woman, quiet and ladylike, in a 'little black dress', and spoke little. Of course she wouldn't, in his presence. He knew the social world of Europe well – he had been Press Attaché to the British Embassy in Italy. He might well have made friendly enquiries about her family. It must have been a narrow squeak for the Countess, but she did not lose her nerve.

When Ruth visited the prison just before Christmas 1961, Bower pushed a little packet towards her, concealed underneath a document. "For you," he murmured. Ruth was a little disconcerted, because she was not supposed to take anything unauthorised out of the prison. When she was able to examine it she found it was a charming little Victorian book of verses, *The Language of Flowers*, with pretty coloured illustrations, which he had bound in beautiful red leather. There was an inscription inside – *MRE from DEB*.

Over Christmas, the Castle was in the safe hands of the Waters, but the lack of any security precautions was a constant nightmare to Ruth. She had at least done her best and had replaced the missing shutters. Those replacements had a sad history. They had come from one of the finest eighteenth century houses in Queen Anne Street.

One day Ruth had noticed that the old house was being demolished – for re-development. "What are you doing with the shutters?" she asked. "The bonfire," said the Foreman, mournfully, one of the old school who disliked destroying good craftsmanship. He let us have them for a fiver, but it cost a lot more than that to adapt them for the Castle.

It was an icy Christmas. Bower told Ruth that it was 42 degrees in his cell – how he knew I do not know. He was quite matter of fact and uncomplaining about it. Ruth thought another such winter might kill him. Perhaps that was what the Home Office hoped. For Beaumont informed Ruth just at this time that the Home Office annual review of sentences had been completed, and in spite of the recommendation of the prison authorities, Bower was not to be released. Ruth had told him previously that if the sentence were not reviewed she had her own plans for making an appeal. Beaumont advised her to go ahead. It could do no harm, he said.

Beaumont had already told Denys of the Home Office's decision, for he had been continually enquiring about it. But Beaumont had also already told him that Ruth had plans to deal with the refusal, and this had completely satisfied him. He was not a bit cast down. He was sure Ruth would succeed.

So Ruth put into action the strategy she had devised, and with the documents she sent a letter reminding Lord Kilmuir of his promise to her, saying that she did not ask for help for herself, but for the grave predicament of a client.

She outlined Bower's case. She said his sentence was now undergoing its annual review – she did not mention that this had already been completed, as she wished to give the Home Office the possibility of a bit of face-saving – and said that there were certain aspects of the medical report that should be brought to the attention of the Home Secretary urgently. If after considering the analysis of the medical report he thought it of sufficient gravity, she asked him to pass it directly to the Home Secretary.

The reply came by return. Lord Kilmuir thought the case so serious that he had handed the report to the Home Secretary with the comment that he knew the writer of it, and had the highest respect for her judgement.

So Ruth had shot her bolt. She had not mentioned the unfair conduct of the whole case, as this would only raise other matters and cause delay, and she needed a quick result. The Home Office could not justify the medical report – no arguing about that. Moreover, the Home Office officials had to justify themselves to the Home Secretary – possibly a fair review of the case had never been put before him.

Ruth had told Denys of what she was doing, so he was full of hope. He also had another treat to remember and think about. The Home Office had permitted another visit to Chiddingstone at the beginning of February – fortunately it had been arranged before Ruth made her appeal. He suspected that some of the swords had been stolen, as an unauthorised dealer had been allowed access to them, who was well known for his thieving activities. He had met the Waters and had been much impressed by them. He also met Mankelow, who afterwards complained bitterly to Ruth that Denys had left without saying goodbye to him. Beaumont had again provided a very sympathetic guardian, who remarked to Ruth as they were preparing to leave, "He shouldn't be going back!"

Eighteen

We continued our weekly visits to the Castle. It never closed. It was open to visitors on winter Sundays – not that many came, but every half crown counted. We had a new urgency in getting Denys' apartment ready, for surely it would soon be needed.

At Easter the new season opened. The place was at least in much better shape than it had been for years. Shabby it might be, but it was clean and polished. Mrs Waters had persuaded Mrs Veall, the wife of the game-keeper, to help with the domestic work. The two Veall boys also came and helped with visitors. David, the elder, was a very responsible boy of 14. Whenever he saw visitors sidling off into the grounds without paying, he was after them like a hare. "2/6!" he would say, firmly blocking their way. "But we only want to go round the grounds..." "2/6," said David, proffering a ticket. No-one escaped him.

It was quite evident that the Castle had become known as a free for all. Some of the scroungers were quite well-heeled. Once Ruth spotted a gentleman and his family strolling through the grounds. Ruth offered him a ticket but he refused to pay. "If you came to Canada you would be welcome in the House of God and would not be asked to pay."

"But," said Ruth, "this is not the House of God, and God does not pay for its maintenance." The reverend gentleman was huffy and said he would complain to the Rector, which he did. The Rector of Chiddingstone wrote complaining to Denys, who replied with an abject apology. Ruth was very angry with him – he said his reply was intended as deep sarcasm. The trouble is that deep sarcasm is not often understood. Anyway, Denys had to live with the Rector after his return home, and they did become quite good friends.

The routine of prison visits went on. On one occasion, Denys Bower gave a little packet to Ruth for safe custody – Anna's letters to him during their engagement. They were important, because they confirmed all he had said about her deception. It had been suggested at the trial that the 'Countess' was a figment of his imagination. At some future date, he said, they could be produced to prove he was right. He never asked for their return. They were immature in style, and rather dull, though she once got stroppy and threatened to break off the engagement. Perhaps this misled him when he really did so; he thought persuasion would bring her round as before. She threw in a French word or two, for a little local colour. Poor Denys! If only he had paid a little more attention to French at school, he would have been suspicious of a 'French' woman who had referred to "*ma coeur.*"

Six weeks had passed since Ruth had sent in her appeal. Not a murmur from the Home Office. Ruth was becoming very anxious. It was not so much Bower's long-term future that was at stake. So far as that was concerned there were other more desperate steps which might be taken, if this method or approach failed. The Council of Civil Liberties, for instance; highly undesirable as it would involve publicity which would be psychologically damaging for Bower. The Press, always game for a bash at authority, would have fun with every word of that medical report. Ruth hoped that the Home Office realised this. No, it was the short-term future that was at stake. When Ruth had received Lord Kilmuir's letter she had briefed Helenus Milmo QC as Leading Counsel. He was Denys Bower's choice; with him, Denys believed he was bound to win – provided of course that he had a reputation to lose.

One Saturday morning, when we were at Chiddingstone, Ruth was called to the telephone. It was Beaumont from Wormwood Scrubs. He had just been informed by the Home Office that Denys Bower was to be released the following November. It was safe to go ahead with the action – now due to come on within the next few weeks.

It was immaterial that the release was not to be immediate. The reason for the delay was the Home Office's custom – when remitting a sentence they always allowed six months for 'rehabilitation'. During this time he would be allowed one week's home leave, and would be permitted to leave the prison each day to take up an approved employment. In this case 'rehabilitation' was unnecessary, but in fact – though this was not the Home Office's kindly intention – it did help with the libel case. If news of Denys Bower's pending release could be kept secret and only revealed at the trial, it would be a nasty shock for the defendants.

The review of the sentence was not, however, a free pardon. He was to be released on licence only, so that at any time he could be recalled by the Home Office if they were not satisfied with his behaviour. Ruth had intended to take up this point later, to get the condition removed. But Denys settled down quietly and happily and she let the matter pass.

When Ruth saw him on the following Monday he was a changed man. His old self had returned, completely blocking out the prison sentence. He was jubilant but quiet, thought the Home Office delay unreasonable, but was not unduly dismayed by it. He had been making his plans. He still had a quantity of Jacobite pamphlets to bind, and six months would give him just enough time to complete the work. He would work full out – after every visit Ruth was to leave with a load of pamphlets. When the news of his release became known after the case, the instructor helped too. After the loss of his best pupil, he left the prison service.

Nineteen

The last stages in the preparation of the case were now occupying much of Ruth's time. Granville Wingate (later Judge Wingate, and one of the trustees of the DEB Bequest) had been instructed, and had advised on the presentation of the case. It was expected to come on early in June, at the beginning of the term. So we had arranged our holiday for the end of June, thinking that would give him a safe margin. But we were wrong!

Ruth had decided early on that Bower should see Milmo in Chambers. Strictly speaking this meeting was not necessary. But Bower had been out of the world for five years. Appearance in Court is daunting for anyone. He, Ruth feared, might break down, haunted by memories of his experience at the Old Bailey. The visit to Milmo would give him his first experience of freedom, and of the normal social world.

Ruth had to apply direct to the Home Office for this concession. Miss X, the Home Office Official with whom Ruth dealt, dismissed it out of hand. Quite unnecessary, she said. Ruth urged the extreme importance of the visit for Bower. Well then, said Miss, let Milmo visit him at the prison. She would make suitable arrangements for that.

"Quite impractical and out of the question," said Ruth, and added that if Miss X did not agree she would have to make application to a higher authority.

"Do not threaten me, Miss Eldridge."

"I am not threatening, I am simply telling you what I am going to do." Miss X knew what Ruth could and would do. Permission for the visit was given.

The Home Office were still evidently continuing their policy of obstruction in any action that might assist Denys. Perhaps they were really annoyed at having revision of his sentence virtually forced on them, and were getting their pound of flesh. DEB with Ruth and two prison officers went off in a taxi to Chambers. The girls in the office were prepared for his visit – they gave him a royal welcome and a sumptuous tea. When Ruth went out into the office she found him chatting happily, very charming and debonair. He had a very useful discussion with Milmo. The exercise was completely successful.

However, he was not so fortunate with his two other applications to Authority. One concerned dental treatment. Two of his front teeth had been crowned, and a few weeks before the case was due he confided to Ruth that they seemed decidedly wobbly. To appear in Court minus two front teeth would be a handicap as well as a distressing disfigurement, for it would make it difficult or impossible to speak clearly. The treatment was not within the scope of prison dentistry. Difficult cases were usually sent to the Dental School at University College Hospital, but they were on vacation at this time. However, Ruth knew the sub-dean – he was a relative – and she appealed to him for advice. He was a compassionate man and was so moved by the case that he offered to make a special visit to the Hospital and carry out the work himself. The prison authorities gave their consent – all was well, until at the last moment the doctor intervened and said the work could be done perfectly well by the prison dentist. Of course no treatment could be given there. So Denys had to be very careful how he chewed, and the teeth held until the day after the case was over. The prison doctor said Denys could now spend some of his damages on dental treatment.

(After Denys' death we found a curious note amongst his papers – a mock will, the bitterest thing he ever wrote, directed mainly against Binney. But it ended on a comical note. He bequeathed his teeth to the Nation, adding an explanatory note to the Will, saying it was these teeth which gave him his devilish grin, followed by an imagined press comment:- *The British Dental Association said, "we are glad these teeth are leaving the country."* Years later Bill Tilley – trustee of the Bequest and Christie's Japanese art expert gave us the explanation of the devilish grin. At a certain auction Bower was bidding for a Japanese sword against Clement Milward, a dealer and collector. Bower outbid Milward and grinned at him triumphantly. Milward was convulsed with rage and shouted, "He's grinning at me! His devilish grin." The more Milward shouted, the more Denys grinned).

The other episode also concerned health – this time his eyesight. He needed glasses for reading but preferred to use a monocle. The time came for the prescription to be renewed – in prison. The Home Office said the system could not provide a monocular lens. Denys entered into a correspondence with them – partly out of devilment. Why, he said, if they were willing to provide two lenses, would they not provide one, which would be cheaper. (Actually the monocle would be dearer though the Home Office did not say this. Perhaps they did not know.) But all that officialdom would supply was a pair of spectacles with round lenses, too small for him, which made him look like Billy Bunter.

Twenty

There was one outstanding matter which Ruth wished to clear up. She knew that the Home Office were concerned that he might try to meet Anna again and that this would lead to trouble – a situation to be avoided at all costs as he was to be released only on licence. He showed no inclination to renew the acquaintance, but Ruth wished to be sure. So when she was sending the petition to Lord Kilmuir she asked Denys, if she procured his release, to promise never to see Anna again. He agreed, but said that she still had the engagement ring, that he must get it back, and he supposed he would have to see her to do that. Ruth said she would get the ring back herself – that would obviate any need for him to see her. She asked if he had any idea where she could find her and he suggested sending a letter to the dental surgery where she had once been a receptionist.

Ruth wrote off at once, asking Anna to get in touch with her. She did not say why, hoping that perhaps curiosity might elicit some response, but for some weeks there was no reply. Then one morning, Anna came on the telephone. Ruth said to her that as all relationships between her and Mr Bower were at an end, he wished her to return the engagement ring. Silence. Then she said she had sold it. She had needed the money because things had been very bad for her after the trial. Somehow Ruth guessed that she was lying, and after some pressure Anna agreed that she still had the ring, and would return it. She suggested meeting Ruth at a small café in Fleet Street.

When Ruth looked up the location of the café, she found that it was just opposite the offices of the *Daily Telegraph*. Was it to be a confrontation with the Press? Well she had no choice. She just had to chance it and go. Anna might not even turn up.

So Ruth set off on her strange assignment. As she left the bus stop in Fleet Street she glanced warily at the offices of the *Daily Telegraph*. All was quiet. All was quiet too in the little café – only a solitary figure sitting at a table in the window. The involuntary thought that passed through Ruth's mind was, "Is this the face that launched a thousand ships?" Anna was certainly no Helen of Troy. She just looked mousey. Rather a disappointing femme fatale.

Yes, she said, in answer to Ruth's query, she was Anna. Ruth ordered coffee and sat down. Anna began to cry quietly. Things had been very difficult for her after the trial. At the first convenient moment, Ruth asked Anna if she had the ring. She produced it and handed it over without a word. She did not ask for payment which Ruth had been prepared to make. Then Anna stood up and said she must go. She had never asked after Denys, never even mentioned him. It was a pretty little antique ring, still in its original box. The diamonds were small but clustered elegantly in a rosette.

So Ruth told Denys she had succeeded in recovering the ring, so that all ties between him and Anna were ended. Soon after his release he asked for the ring. Ruth wondered if he wanted to keep it as a sad memento, but a few days later he told her he had sold it. He was no sentimentalist, and usually only kept things if he wanted them as part of his collections – or if he just forgot to throw them away. He was badly in need of pocket money at the time, and was quite ready to capitalize on anything superfluous.

Twenty-One

By now the case was nearly on us. And then, during the week before it was due to come on the *Sunday Pictorial* asked for leave to amend its pleadings and increase the payment into Court. When such an application is granted it is a condition that the applicant pays the costs of the proceedings up to that date. This is only fair as the other side will have incurred much expense. So Ruth at once sent off the briefs to Milmo and Wingate, with the fees marked on them, so that their fees would at least be covered. The *Sunday Pictorial* had originally entered a plea of fair comment, and that they had apologised, and that the plaintiff had suffered no damage. They had paid £100 into Court – a derisory sum.

They must have felt that their pleadings were a bit thin. They now wished to add that they had acted upon information coming from a usually reliable source. This raised an interesting point. In the past, when the Press used confidential information, they had claimed that they should not be obliged to disclose its source. Otherwise, they argued, no-one would ever say anything in confidence again, and this might on occasion be against the public interest. The popular press is singularly devoted to the public interest. However, those were cases where the evidence was incidental, not where it formed part of the pleadings. The amendment was welcomed by Bower's Counsel. The defendant increased the payment into Court to £212.68 – contemptuous damages again. The real problem arises when the payment is realistic, but less than you hope to win. For then even if you win but are awarded damages the same or less than this sum you pay all costs incurred after the payment into Court.

But the case did not come on the following week, nor the week after. The preceding case dragged on and on, and did not end until the very day we were due to travel to Scotland. So we spent the first two days of our holiday in Court – and very exciting it was too. The morning of the trial was fine and sunny. With luck, we thought, the trial would end that day. So we packed our bags and left everything to set off that evening.

Denys Bower had arrived at the Court without incident. Not a word had leaked out about his impending release. This had been Ruth's great worry – it would have completely spoilt the impact of the news at the trial.

He was accompanied by two duennas, carefully selected as usual by Beaumont. They were a pleasant couple – not in uniform – who behaved with great consideration and discretion. To an outsider, they were simply supportive friends of the plaintiff.

Denys Bower was looking spruce and cheerful. He appeared to be in remarkably good health and showed no ill effects from his long incarceration. He greeted me as an old friend. He did not remember me, but he knew about all I had done at Chidd.

He had asked Ruth urgently to bring him a nip of brandy, to give him moral support. When Ruth produced a little flask Milmo looked horrified, but Ruth murmured it was little more than coloured water. Denys downed it with great satisfaction – his enforced abstinence had been so prolonged that he had evidently forgotten the taste of neat brandy.

We had to wait for an hour or so before going into Court, for several matters from the previous day had to be cleared up. And even when we were actually in Court several legal preliminaries had to be settled: the vital question of whether the *Sunday Pictorial* must divulge the source of the information on which the libellous statements were based.

Leading Counsel for the defendant was Bernard Gillies. Rather an odd choice, for he was not a libel expert, more an Old Bailey type, and somewhat old-fashioned at that – aggressive and hectoring. Perhaps having seen Denys Bower at a state of collapse in his trial, they thought it would only be necessary to bash him down and demoralize him. Then they would point to the wreckage and say: look at him! What reputation has he to lose? If so they were in for a shock.

Milmo was the antithesis of Gillies – quiet, incisive, extremely courteous – in cross-examination he was matchless. He was like an intelligent terrier – missing nothing, tracking down the faintest scent – he must have caused instant apprehension in those who had something to hide.

The judge, Mr Justice Megaw, was not a libel expert, but he was extremely careful in his handling of the case. Much time for instance, was taken over the question of the source of the information. Gillies pressed the point that if there were no confidentiality, the Press were bound to be deprived of useful sources of information. However in the end, Megaw ruled that the *Sunday Pictorial* must disclose. So Denys Bower made legal history, for his case is now the authority on this point.

Gillies had hinted that the source was very important – something to do with Scotland Yard. We could hardly wait for it to be revealed.

And so at last, battle commenced.

Milmo opened the case. He first announced that Denys Bower was to be released from Prison later in the year. He gave the news very quietly, almost as an understatement. Of course, it put a very different complexion on the whole case.

Perhaps Gillies reflected bitterly that the *Sunday Pictorial* was dismally lacking in professional expertise, in failing to ferret out the news. It meant he ought to re-align his approach to the case; but really it was too late for him to do anything effective.

Milmo outlined the circumstances of the alleged libel, which he did very concisely. Then Denys went into the witness box.

He behaved impeccably. His natural manner was diffident and rather engaging. He once confessed to Ruth that really he was rather nervous. But like many nervous people, he was liable to put on an aggressive act if someone tried to ruffle him. This was the danger in the witness box,, and when it came to cross-examination Gillies did in fact try to needle him. In vain!

First he tried to denigrate Denys' achievements. "You were just a shop keeper," he almost sneered.

"Yes," agreed Denys with modest pride. "At number 2 Baker Street."

It was rather a fortunate gambit from our point of view, for it established Denys in the mind of the jury, not as a wealthy 'castle owner,' and persecutor of helpless girls, but as an ordinary person trying to make a living, and driven out of business and home by the big developers. Then Gillies referred to the trial, going into it in some detail. Denys did not show any anger, but just the right amount of personal indignation. He had been tried once, did he have to go into it all again? The judge said that the defence was entitled to ask such questions. Thus encouraged, Gillies proceeded along the same lines. At one point Denys protested his innocence. Gillies pounced in his best Bailey manner. "Be careful," he said, "you are committing perjury. These papers may be sent to the Director of Public Prosecutions."

The judge intervened quietly, saying "He did not plead guilty. Believing in one's innocence is not perjury." This rather took the wind out of Gillies' sails. After some rather ineffective bullying the cross-examination was over. Denys returned to his seat by my side in the Court.

By lunchtime Milmo had finished presenting his case. We all, including the prison officers, went out and had lunch in the Court's restaurant. Granville Wingate joined us, but Milmo had other business. There were about a dozen of us altogether – I think some from Chambers must have joined us. They were popping in and out of Court all the time, to see how things were going. The Law Courts restaurant was not exactly a gastronomical treat, but we were a very merry party. Denys Bower was in high spirits, his ordeal over, and was quite the host. Lunch over, we all trooped back into Court.

Gillies opened the defence. He was given to histrionics. One of the points he had made in his cross-examination was that public attitudes to mental instability had become more understanding. Therefore an inference that someone was mentally unstable would not make him a social untouchable, as it might have done in the past. Denys had amiably agreed, but had pointed out that mental problems were not yet a social recommendation. Gillies returned to this tactic.

He pleaded that if Denys were indeed mad, he should never have been sentenced, and therefore the *Sunday Pictorial* article was doing him a service by drawing public attention to his plight. They were trying to see that justice was done.

There were two defence witnesses. The first, Catlin, the reporter who had garnered the tale, was a quiet middle-aged man. He said his information had come from an important source, to disclose it would be harmful to future relations; would it be sufficient if he wrote it down and gave it to the judge? The judge read the note, passed it to Counsel and said that the information must be disclosed in open Court.

This was the secret we had been awaiting so eagerly. He had got the story from a policeman in a pub off Whitehall. Not a hundred yards from Scotland Yard, it is true.

The second witness was the Crime Editor, who had been

responsible for the production of the article. He entered the witness box with supreme confidence, ready to put the Court at its ease. We learned afterwards that he had a reputation as a charmer. Under cross-examination his aplomb was unshakeable. No, he said, there had been no time to check with the Home Office the accuracy of the police statement. It was Saturday – there was no-one at the Home Office – the article had to come out the next day – the following Sunday would not do – it was in the public interest to publish immediately. What he meant by 'public interest' even Milmo could not elicit. (Did he really mean pro bono public, or did he just mean that the public had an insatiable appetite for news, which of course it was in the *Sunday Pictorial's* interest to gratify?) As for the position of the apology: Milmo asked why it had not been given the importance of a front-page position. "Well," said the Editor, "the importance of the front page tends to be exaggerated – some readers go straight to the back." Then why not the back page? Some readers go straight to the sports page. "Every inch," he said, warming to his theme, "every inch of the *Sunday Pictorial* is important." And he claimed the apology had appeared on the most widely read page in the paper, under the most famous cartoon in the world.

"And what cartoon is that?" Milmo asked mildly. The ever watchful terrier had uncannily seen his opportunity and pounced.

Then a very strange thing happened. The Crime Editor's face crumpled like a burst balloon. He stuttered. The name of the cartoon had slipped his memory. A titter fluttered through the court and then immediately died away. Milmo did not exploit the triumph. He handed the relevant page to the Crime Editor almost sympathetically, to refresh his memory, and copies were also given to the jury. It was the Andy Capp cartoon.

The unfortunate Freudian blockage made clear beyond all

pretence the flimsy nature of the defence. Wriggle as they might they had been cornered. The Crime Editor tried to make a brave show, but he could not retrieve his mask.

We did not leave for Scotland that night. The case was to continue next day. We bundled into a taxi with Denys and the prison officers. They dropped us at Wimpole Street, and continued on to Wormwood Scrubs. It was the most adventurous beginning to a holiday we could have had.

Twenty-Two

Next day we were back in Court. Gillies addressed the jury, and then Milmo. Then the judge summed up. He took quite a time over this, for he was very careful, as he had been all through the case. This was to our advantage, for if we did get a favourable verdict, the defendant could hardly appeal on the grounds that the jury had been misdirected.

Then at last the jury retired. They were quite a long time considering their verdict. They must have been out for nearly an hour. Denys must have remembered the last occasion when his fate depended on the jury, and the dreadful result. However he maintained his sangfroid.

Then at last the jury returned, and we all filed back into our seats. The jury had found for the plaintiff. In all, damages amounted to about £9,750. The jury had worked it all out very carefully – that was why they had been so long, no doubt.

You have to multiply this sum at least ten times to get the value in today's money. The defendants were outraged – said they would appeal, but Milmo doubted whether they would. He was very grateful with the result.

The press was there, including the *Times* official reporter. Ruth gave him all the necessary information and papers, to make sure he got the report right, for this case would be an authority on disclosure of sources of information. The popular press gave only a bare report of the case. They refrained from making capital out of the discomfiture of the Crime Editor, a restraint they had never extended to Denys Bower.

Then we hurried off. Denys and the prison officers left by a private exit to avoid the press – though I think the popular press out of respect for their disgraced colleague, would have avoided him. I last remember seeing him going downstairs, waving goodbye and crying "Have a good holiday! Forget about Chiddingstone! Forget about Bower!" That was a fruitless injunction: the next exciting instalment of the Chiddingstone saga could never be far from our minds.

For Ruth this was not the end of the case. There were still all the costs to be settled. We had of course been awarded costs, but these had to be taxed. That is, she had to attend before a Taxing Master, an official who would settle what charges were reasonable. It was notorious that some Taxing Masters were very difficult, so, to avoid any party claiming that discrimination had been shown against them, you had to ballot for your Taxing Master. You had to take the luck of the draw – and Ruth drew Master Hood. She groaned. He was the most dreaded of them all.

She had to place all the papers before him, so that he had adequate information on which to base the costs. The first thing he picked on was Wingate's original assessment of probable damages. "£1,000," mused Master Hood. "You must have been very pleased with your damages."

"But," Ruth pointed out, "that was before Denys Bower was granted his release. That put a different complexion on the whole matter."

Master Hood was not appeased. Gillies, he pointed out, had only £250 on his brief. This was a straightforward case, insisted Master Hood – no need to call in Milmo. But, protested Ruth, the progress of the case, and its outcome, showed that it was far from simple.

"No," insisted Master Hood again, "Wingate could have managed perfectly well on his own. He is a very experienced lawyer, and ..." he added thoughtfully, for he was also a yachtsman "... a very good helmsman too." And then, in spite of Ruth's protests, he very unsportingly halved Milmo's and Wingate's fees.

Ruth was so incensed that she put the matter before the Law Society. They finally said that if she felt like that she had better appeal. Now it is unusual to appeal against a Master's decision. If no accommodation is reached, the case then goes to appeal. But Master Hood was adamant: what he had spoken, he had spoken.

So the case went to appeal. Ruth won her main points. The case was returned to Master Hood for reconsideration. Probably to save his face, he did not conclude quite everything, but substantially she was satisfied.

All this took about six months, and in the course of the negotiations she got to know the solicitors on the other side quite well. One morning, over a genial cup of coffee, she asked them why they had put in such a peculiar (and risky) defence. She knew that they were the second firm who had acted in the case, so there must have been some disagreement with the first firm. It was all Cecil King's idea, they said – he was the proprietor of the *Sunday Pictorial*. He dictated the line they were to follow. Left to themselves they would have handled the case rather differently. He also fixed the amount of damages to be paid into Court, saying if Bower got a penny more than £200 he would go through the roof. (It is a pleasant thought, Cecil King flying heavenwards above Fleet Street like a meteor.) Ah well, God does indeed move in mysterious ways.

Ruth also picked up one or two other small amounts in damages as a result of the action. These were from minor papers that had repeated the libel. One of them apologised and said that it had been an administrative error. The Bower file was marked red, which meant that the matter was forbidden material and should not be touched. For a year Ruth had a cuttings service which gave everything published about Denys Bower. Quite a lot of files must have been marked red. All in all, she got nearly £12,000 which paid off the Bank and all other debts. Sinclair also put in a claim. When his fees had been settled it was agreed that payment should be made in instalments. Could they now be paid in full, he asked. Ruth took great pleasure in refusing.

Twenty-Three

Denys Bower returned to prison to serve out the rest of his time, apart from a week's special home leave. By rights, he should have been released daily to work at some approved employment, to prepare him for his life in the great world. Ruth had in fact been able to arrange something for him. A client of the firm, a distinguished antiquarian bookseller, had a book bindery, where he agreed Denys might work. Denys was looking forward to it, especially as he would have the opportunity of using some tools which were not available in prison. But in the end he declined because he feared he would be perpetually hounded by the Press. His prospective employer was much relieved – he foresaw the work of his bookbindery being disrupted. The Home Office made no comment about his decision.

Denys was always prepared to look on the brighter side of life, and he saw it was really much more use to him to get on with the rebinding of his Jacobite pamphlets especially as his instructor promised to give him all the help that he could. At this time Denys was all enthusiasm for book-binding and had plans for setting up a workshop at Chiddingstone; but in fact after his release he never touched the work again.

Denys worked away happily, and his spirits were also raised by the renewal of an old acquaintance – with his friend Steve Valline. Steve was an American, an engineer who had been working in London at the end of the war. He too was a collector, and one day he had wandered into Denys' shop. Denys, he at once realised, did not like Americans. But Steve had taken a liking to him, and made up his mind that he would make Denys like HIM. He did so, and the two became good friends, and had many antiquarian jaunts together. (He learned that Denys' initial disapproval had been caused by an American General, who had just left the shop. He had made Denys turn out the place, made some disparaging remarks, and left without buying anything.)

Eventually, Steve's work took him out of London, and he lost touch with Denys. He wrote many times, but his letters were never answered. Then when he was visiting a Wild West tourist Mecca, he sent Denys one of their special postcards. He later told Ruth that he remembered it with a shudder. It was headed "Wanted, dead or alive." Below was a picture of a gallows with a hangman's noose. In the noose you drew the head of the person you wished to contact. Fortunately this card, like other letters, was never received by Denys.

When Steve returned to London he sought out Denys, with no success. His shop and home were obliterated. He at last found out what had happened when he was visiting an antiques fair. He asked one of the stall holders if he knew what had become of Denys Bower and was told the story. He was thunderstruck. The whole affair was so thoroughly out of character with Denys.

He got in touch with Wormwood Scrubs, and was told he must get a visitor's permit from Denys. But when Steve tried to get in touch with him the message was garbled, Denys thought it was someone from the Press trying to get an interview, and refused the permit. Steve, not to be put off, wrote indignantly: is this the way to treat an old friend? Then

Denys understood, saw Valline and put him in touch with Ruth. The two old friends remained in touch until Denys' death, and Steve and his wife visited him at the Castle. This is just one example of the deep attachment Denys could inspire in those who understood and valued him.

Twenty-Four

Denys' special leave week was fixed for September. The flat was all ready for him. We had done the best we could with our limited means. It had been made clean and comfortable – new electric stove and kitchen equipment. We hoped he would know how to use them. The antique furniture – and he had some fine stuff – had all been polished.

The plan was that Ruth would fetch him from the prison at 8 o'clock in the morning – the usual time for commencement of leave. She would bring him back to Wimpole Street where he would have breakfast. She would arrange an appointment for him with our dentist in Harley Street; and then at midday she would drive him down to Chiddingstone, stopping for lunch at the New Fantail at Farnborough. It was a quiet place and conveniently located on the A21.

The date had been kept a dead secret, in view of the unwelcome attention from the Press. But when Ruth arrived at the prison, she was told that reporters had been lying in wait since 6 o'clock. Someone had tipped them off. This was quite a common occurrence – it was a miracle that the date of his release had not leaked out prematurely.

Beaumont had a suggestion. At the left of the prison gates was a little side alley. If Ruth turned directly into this she would connect with the road further on, bypassing the Press waiting outside the main entrance. It would give her just a few seconds start.

The car was loaded up, the boot filled to capacity with the rebound pamphlets. Denys said approvingly that he admired a woman who did not worry about the springs of her car. True, it was a tough car – one of the splendid old Riley 1 ½ litres, and they quite liked a good weight at the back. Denys was placed well back on the rear seat. Cars did not have all round glazing as they do now, and the rear window was provided with a blind. Ruth pulled this down. It meant that her rear view was blocked which made driving difficult – and rather dangerous – but it prevented the possibility of photographs being taken through the rear window. She found an old copy of *The Times* on the floor and Denys buried his head in that.

All was ready. Ruth started the engine, revved up in first gear, ready for a racing start. The Riley could beat even a Jag in first gear. She turned the steering wheel into the left lock. The gatekeeper called, "Now!" the prison gates clanged open and she was off. She got off to a good start, but alas, lost the benefit a little later when she missed her way. At the traffic lights she found herself alongside a press car. One of the reporters tapped on her window.

"Give us a photograph," he said. "We'll get you in the end!"

"Not now or ever," called Ruth, and was away as the lights changed. She knew the back streets of the area better than the Press, and eluded them again. At the next set of lights she glanced sideways, and saw the press car which had taken the road parallel to hers and was waiting at the cross roads. The chase was getting too dangerous. She was just getting out her purse, and was about to tell Denys to get out, get a cab and go to Wimpole Street, when the press car moved off. She waited, and when she judged that they must be well on their way she made her way home without further trouble.

The Press, realising they had lost the scent, went on to Chiddingstone, where of course there was no sign of Denys. They had to content themselves with a short paragraph saying Denys Bower had been released on home leave, and been fetched from prison by a fair-headed woman and driven to an unknown destination.

In the meantime I had been waiting anxiously at home, putting off my departure for the office as long as possible. Presently I heard the front door open and footsteps on the stairs. I went and opened our flat door. There was Denys, rather flustered and breathless. He dropped into an armchair and began the story of his adventure. Ruth had dropped him at the front door and given him her key, so that he could get in while she garaged the car. I had to tear myself away – the office could wait no longer, and leave Mama to give him breakfast. It smelled delicious.

He went off to the dentist in Harley Street later that morning to have some first aid done on his tooth. Our dentist was a Geordie, and a character in his own right. They got on famously and Denys became a permanent patient.

Ruth collected him at lunchtime. They had lunch at the New Fantail as arranged, it was a great disappointment. Ruth had hoped that his first celebration would be something of a treat. They made their way quietly to the Castle – and it was a really quiet backwater then. The Press had all gone away and they gave no trouble at all during the week's home leave.

We went down to him the following Sunday. As we drew up at the South Entrance we were rather alarmed to see him emerge from the south field, very red in the face. We thought he was taking more violent exercise than was good for him, after so many years of inactivity. The south field was infested with thistles and he was digging them up, one by one. The only way to get rid of them, he said. He used to come up with odd bits of domestic and gardening lore like this; things he must have learned as a child, and he always observed them. He kept just one thistle, which grew to over six feet. Then someone, to his grief, cut it down. Just as well, for it might have re-infected the whole field. That was the end of the thistles – they never returned.

Our parents had both come with us. Denys had met not only my mother, but also my father, who had stayed to talk to him while he was having breakfast. When he rose to go, saying he must go to the office, Denys jumped up, shook hands warmly and said, "I hope we meet again soon, sir. I am sure we shall be good friends."

Ruth, who was present, smiled to herself. My father made very few friends. He was the kindest of men, but he was a great wit and got bored with people very easily unless they were of the same quick turn of mind. But he did take a liking to Denys, who never committed that unforgiveable sin of being a bore. He came to have a great influence over him. He only had to say, "Denys, you can't do that ..." and Denys didn't. He regarded my father I think, with the same respect and affection that he had for his grandfather – who seemed to have much more influence over him than his own father.

We took Denys out for a run in the car. We told him he must sit well back in his seat and not get out. When going through Southborough we passed a little antique / junk shop that Denys had known. He wanted to get out and look, but we drove on. We had to stop at the next traffic lights; he jumped out and ran back to look.

Then he went back to prison. It was stupid of the Home Office to insist on going by the book. Perhaps they thought it would be good for him, or perhaps – more likely – they did not think at all. At any rate, he enjoyed a very useful bout of intensive book-binding – at the taxpayer's expense.

Denys was to be released early in November, but the date was not made public. During this time nothing much happened. Ruth was pursuing an action against Binney for the return of the Japanese lacquer writing box from the famous Seymour Trower Collection. He relinquished it in the end.

When the time came for the release, Ruth talked things over with our parents. She wanted at all costs to keep Denys away from the Press. Once they got hold of him they could put on him what pressure they liked. His fragile self-confidence would not stand up to their manoeuvres, and they would not care what sort of fool they made him look. His great friend Colonel Munro had written to him, urging him to keep out of the clutches of the Press. As a journalist, he said, he was only too well acquainted with their tactics. Ruth thought it would be better if he did not return to Chiddingstone immediately. So our parents agreed that she could bring him straight back to Wimpole Street, and he should spend a few days quietly there, until the hue and cry died down.

We unfortunately had no spare room. The rooms in the flat were spacious but limited in number. But he could have a camp bed in the corner of the sitting room, and during the day it could be concealed by a screen. It may seem strange that our parents should so readily agree to entertain a person whom they had met only twice for a few hours. But they felt they knew him well. For the past eighteen months we had talked of little else but his affairs. It was in the evening that Ruth brought his papers to sort out. It was as if the hero in a novel had suddenly come to life.

Ruth did not tell Denys of this arrangement. He assumed that he would be taken down to Chiddingstone on the morning of his release – usually at 9am, to be brought forward to 8am in Denys' case, to avoid any possible risk of confrontation with the Press. But on the day before the release Beaumont telephoned Ruth. The Press had got wind of the date, for reporters had been telephoning the prison constantly: the date must have leaked out, for they were asking if it were true. This was not an unexpected development. Such leakages occurred. So Beaumont, knowing what had happened at the home leave, had persuaded the Home Office to release Denys at midnight, which he had pointed out to them was really the same day.

Later he telephoned again, to say that the Governor and he did not at all like the idea of Ruth driving about Kent in the small hours, possibly being harassed by the Press, so they had decided to drive Denys down themselves. Ruth explained that other arrangements had been made, which would put the Press off the scent.

Again Beaumont telephoned. The Press were being very persistent, so the Governor and he had decided, off their own bat, that Denys should be released at 10.30 that night. Only the Governor, Ruth and he knew of this, he said. "So if the Press get wind of this, it is from one of us!"

When Denys retired at the usual time and was locked up, he knew nothing of these arrangements. Then at about 9 o'clock, he heard someone fumbling with the lock. He recognised Beaumont's voice, cursing the keys. He and the Governor had come to release him, but they were not very handy with the prison equipment.

When eventually they got the door open, Denys was told to get up at once and dress – in less than 2 hours he would be a free man.

In the meantime Ruth was getting ready to set off. At the last moment, my father said he thought he had better go with her, in case there was any trouble. Then my mother insisted on going too. The truth is, she was longing to be chased by the Press. I stayed behind to have hot drinks prepared for the party when they returned.

All was quiet at Wormwood Scrubs – not a sign of the

Press. And so Ruth passed through the prison gates for the last time.

She heard Denys in the distance, chattering away to his escort. Beaumont was there to see him off. Denys seized him by the hand. He kept on wringing Beaumont's hand, thanking him, and chattering away; until at last Beaumont pushed him into the car. As he shut the door, he turned to Ruth, the tears running down his face, and murmured, "You can't help liking the bloody old fool." And that was the best summing up of one's feelings about Denys that I have ever heard.

To my mother's intense disappointment, the return journey was entirely uneventful. The Press did show up eventually, but the bird had flown, and of course they did not find him at Chiddingstone either. They had to content themselves with pointing out that Anna was not to be found at her Peckham address, and leave their readers to draw whatever conclusions they wished. It is strange what trouble the Press took to remind their readers of the existence of Denys Bower.

We had a little folding camp bed ready for him in the sitting room. He arrived talking, and was still talking when he went to bed. Indeed we could still hear him talking when we had all left the room, and we replied to him from different parts of the flat.

Next morning he was up and dressed, with the bed folded tidily away. His impeccably methodical ways gave us quite the wrong impression of his true domestic ways. Perhaps it was the effect of prison discipline. But he had been very well brought up, and we noticed in many things that his childhood memories must have stuck. No doubt his mother had repeated to him: "Never put your host to unnecessary trouble."

Ruth had arranged to take him out on a shopping spree that afternoon. She had set aside enough money to kit him out handsomely, for she was determined that he should not meet his acquaintances looking down and out. He spent the morning indoors, talking to Mama about his life. She was always a good listener, and she reproved him roundly when she thought he deserved it – as he told us later, without rancour. One of his merits was that he expected frankness to be returned with equal frankness. He would accept criticism at its face value, and did not try to work double meanings into it.

Twenty-Five

The story he told was not a particularly happy one. Denys Bower had married twice, disastrously. Until he was thirty-five or so, he had lived contentedly at home. He liked to take a pretty girl out to dinner, and he was a charming host and escort. He also liked family life, but the idea of uniting the two, and organising his own domestic bliss he did not find attractive. Possibly quite a number of men do not – an attitude which is regarded as quite understandable nowadays, but then it was not.

In 1939, he became engaged to a singularly attractive young woman, much younger than he was. Her looks, judging by her photographs, were the ideal fashionable at the time. After two years he still had not come to the point, and she broke off the engagement. It was desperation. She was still fond of him, and had he crawled back repentantly with the date of the wedding fixed, she would probably have forgiven him. Perhaps he did not take her seriously enough. For romance bloomed quickly in those days of the war. She met an army officer, they fell for each other and were married. Denys was furious beyond reason. It was all his fault, he had treated her very badly.

He was in this mood when the Bank seconded him to the branch at Matlock. He was not liable for military service, owing to his disabled right hand, and the Bank must have found it useful to have an experienced clerk who could be moved around as the need arose.

He was quartered in a hotel in Matlock, and there he met with a Jewish family – a mother and her two daughters, the elder (Sylvia Bianca) a young woman in her early twenties, the other still a schoolgirl. They were Italian refugees who had come over from Italy just before the War. They had settled in Hampstead. When the air-raids began, the father (who seems to have been in a prosperous way) sent his womenfolk to safety in Derbyshire.

Denys took to them – they seemed such a jolly family, he said. He took them round the sights of Derbyshire, and must have made life very entertaining for them – especially for Sylvia. For him, the family were merely a pleasant way of passing the time; but she evidently adored him. When they returned to London she corresponded with him. We found her letters amongst his papers after his death. He had not singled them out for preservation, he just kept ALL his correspondence. They were simple letters; she must have been a nice girl. But there was one ominous theme: she kept saying that she hoped to receive a letter from him, but none had come. Alas, her letters moved him so little that we found one unopened.

However, she persevered. Both families were against the match. The Bowers must have had the gloomiest doubts about Denys and his marital responsibilities. A marriage outside the faith cannot have been pleasing to her parents; but Jews are not as entirely adamant about a daughter marrying a non-Jew, as they would be with a son. For they regard the mother as the one who will influence the children, and it is she who will shape their religious upbringing. So they were married – in the Church of England.

Denys was moved to Manchester and they had a little flat there. Sylvia does not seem to have been very happy. She must have been lonely, and the flat not very convenient. It was an upper flat in a converted house, and coal had to be carried up for the fires, a task which Sylvia often had to carry out for herself. When she protested about this ("Quite right too," our Ma interjected) Denys pointed out that she was young and strong, and the elderly lady doctor next door managed very well.

In the end, Sylvia's parents suggested that the young couple should move to London. Her father must have had a shrewd idea of Denys' financial potential, for he suggested that Denys should give up the bank and engage in antique dealing. Denys was not averse. His plan had obvious attractions.

So a decaying antique business was bought, at number 2 Baker Street. Denys put his gratuity from the Bank into it, his father and father-in-law made a contribution, and Denys had enough unwanted items in his collection to stock the shop. He and his bride would have rooms in the in-law's house. Not the best location for the most well-founded marriage; in this case it spelled doom.

Syvia preceded him to London. She wrote to him, telling him she was working hard decorating their room and making everything ready. Perhaps she already saw him as a steadfast member of a Jewish household, for when he arrived in London, he was indeed enmeshed in its coils. Her Jewish male relations, of whom there seemed to be an endless number, descended on Denys and told him how a good Jewish husband should behave.

At work it was no better. His father-in-law had appointed, no doubt wisely, a Jewish accountant to go through the accounts weekly. Now Denys was good at accounts; he resented supervision. Inevitably, in the end there was a ROW. Denys left the paternal home to take up residence in a hotel.

He told his wife she could come with him, or not – just as she liked. She chose to remain at home.

Three years later she issued proceedings for divorce. Denys contested it not because he had the slightest wish to be reunited with Sylvia, but as a matter of principle. She was the one who had been in the wrong. However, she won the day. The defence cost Denys dear, but Sylvia did not claim maintenance. Instead she kept the family silver.

Denys did not re-embark on matrimony for another seven years. Then he met a Danish girl. He must have thought she had domestic inclinations, for he made her a little kitchen on the ground floor of the Portman Square house, and bought her a sewing machine. However, she had other ideas, and that marriage broke up even quicker than the first.

Free from the influence of his family he had a high old time. He made the acquaintance of Lady Victor Paget, a socialite of the thirties. She was probably quite glad to have a personable escort, and no doubt saw that he paid her way. She initiated him into Ascot and other social delights, and became a director of his company Cavendish Hood.

He became the director of a fashionable charity which was set up to provide comforts for the forces during the Korean war, and the committee used to meet at his house. It was in this way that he met Queen Mary's lady-in-waiting, who indicated that Her Majesty would very much like to see his collections. But he feared his establishment was not up to a royal visitation – Queen Mary might make unscheduled sorties into neglected corners – so he did not take up the hint.

It was a past from which he was completely separated. It probably did Denys good to talk so freely. In the afternoon Ruth took him on a shopping spree.

There was enough money for him to buy a handsome trousseau, for she was determined he would make his reappearance into the world in style. They went to Hawkes and Gieves and bought a great coat and suit. He did a dress parade for us that evening, and very handsome he looked. Although he had no exercise in prison, the frugal diet had fined his figure down. Those who had only seen him, a poor bent figure in the dock, would hardly recognise him – indeed he cannot have looked so well for years and years.

He also wanted a new sports jacket and slacks, so next morning Mama took him to John Lewis. They chose a jacket successfully, but Mama said he must try on the slacks, and pushed him, very reluctant into a changing cubicle.

He reappeared almost instantly and said they would do. "You did not have time to try them," said Mama. No, he was too excited, he said. And indeed that was true. When he was out the previous day with Ruth he had taken her hand as they crossed Regent Street, like a child.

Twenty-Six

The Press, Waters told us, were still prowling around Chiddingstone, so it was decided that Denys should remain in town at the weekend and Mama, Ruth and I should go down there. A reporter met Mama in the drive and asked if she were Denys Bower's mother. When she disclaimed that responsibility he just went away quietly. I went up to the village gate to plant some crocuses and a reporter asked me if Denys were at the Castle. When I said no, he went away quietly too. It was a very cold day so perhaps that cooled their professional enthusiasm.

Denys was left to his own devices during the week, and he spent his time walking all over central London. There was one particular objective he was interested in.

Before he was released, he had mentioned to Ruth the necessity for a car. He had kept up his driving licence, so there was no difficulty about that. Ruth agreed it would be difficult to manage without one, but there was no money to spare. Perhaps a small car, said Ruth. "A Rolls," said Denys.

He told her that he once, as a young man, had a sporting Rolls. When he arrived home one evening, he found some workmen had been making a hole just outside the drive entrance, which made access difficult. So he decided to leave the car outside for the night. "Wrap it up well," warned the workmen. A sharp frost was expected. He didn't and there was. The car froze up and that was the end of it. Ruth laughed, and no more was said.

Denys however, went on thinking about it. While he was in prison, he got particulars of second-hand Rolls. He told Ruth he had found a very reasonably priced 1947 Silver Wraith - £650 – advertised by one Mr Palmer, who had a garage somewhere in Fulham, and he had been to see it. Ruth said it would be far too expensive to run, and was quite unrealistic.

On Thursday that week they were invited to lunch at the Westbury Hotel, by Quinn the bank manager, who had authorised the loan to Denys to create the flats. He was a genial person, no doubt very relieved that the Bank had not lost money over the project, and disposed to be generous. So when Denys asked if an advance might be allowed to buy a car, Quinn said he thought that a reasonable request. "£650," asked Denys. Oh yes, Quinn thought that quite a fair sum.

After the lunch was over, Ruth said Denys walked back up to Bond Street in complete silence. He went straight upstairs when they went in, and when Ruth went up at 5 o'clock he was sitting huddled in an armchair like a disconsolate bird. Ruth turned to Mama. "What's wrong?" she asked.

Mama said, "He's sulking. He says you won't let him buy a Rolls." Now Ruth had never put any interdict on the Rolls; she had simply said it was a mad idea. She was fed up, and she said (more or less) you do as you damn well please.

"Oh, may I?" he brightened up like a school boy. "May I go and ring now? There was someone else after it." Fancy a retired antique dealer being taken in by a con like that!

Denys wanted Ruth to go and see the Rolls, but she said

he must arrange the deal himself – she would have nothing to do with it. So he fixed everything up. The car needed some adjustments. So we took Denys to Chiddingstone at the weekend, and when it was ready he would come back to us for a day or two.

Twenty-Seven

But on this second visit Ruth had a nasty moment. Late one afternoon she heard someone at the door. The janitor, Townsend was speaking to them. Townsend was one of the last of an old breed. The doorkeepers in Harley and Wimpole Street used to be men of great dignity. Townsend, a fine old Cockney, revered the firm and took an infinite pride in his job.

She heard them ask, "Does Miss Eldridge live here?"

Townsend replied, with great dignity, "This is Mr Eldridge's residence..." Ruth could not catch the next words. Presently Townsend came into her room. He said the Press (from the *Daily Express*) wanted to see her. He had told them that he did not know whether she was available. They had said that if she was not free they would wait.

Of course everyone in the office knew about the case, but Denys' whereabouts had been kept secret. Townsend probably guessed he was staying at 84 but he would be too discreet to say anything. Ruth braced herself. Denys might be back at any moment. She must see the reporters and get rid of them.

The two strode into her room. One, the reporter, McNeish stood there arrogantly. "Where's Bower?" he demanded. The other, the photographer, who was carrying his gear, looked somewhat dilapidated and smelt strongly of fish and chips.

Ruth said, "Why do you ask me?" McNeish said said he had information that he was living at 84. Ruth remarked, like the Duke of Wellington, "If you believe that, you'll believe anything." McNeish, surprisingly, looked sheepish. He hadn't really believed it, he said, but he would get Bower's story sooner or later, so Ruth might as well give him the information now.

Ruth said that if he would tell her how much he was prepared to pay for the story she would pass the message on, and Mr Bower could decide for himself whether he was prepared to sell it. "We could not do that until we heard the story," said McNeish.

"And then," said Ruth, "you would not pay."

"Why won't you cooperate like other solicitors?" said McNeish. "We shall get the story sometime, anyway."

"Perhaps," said Ruth, "but then it will no longer be news, and will be of no use to you."

After a few more pleasant words the reporters left, leaving behind the smell of fish and chips.

The office was now closed. Only Ruth's partner remained. The waiting room was dark, and she peered from behind the curtains into Wimpole Street. There was a car parked just outside, with a man sitting in it holding a newspaper in front of his face. Another man was walking up and down, and from time to time he stopped and spoke to the man in the car. It was a foggy night, which gave the episode Dickensian eeriness. Then Ruth heard her partner leave. The house was in darkness. The man got into the car and drove off. Five minutes later Ruth heard Denys' key in the door.

Ruth was apprehensive in case any reporter was still hanging round, but there was no further trouble. They had given up the chase. It was remarkable really, that no one had spotted Denys during his daily perambulations.

At last the Rolls was ready for collection. Ruth refused to go up and see it, and Denys drove off to Chiddingstone in solitary splendour.

We saw it at the weekend. It was pale blue below, black above, a Mulliner's body: LPB 1. That model of the Silver Wraith was, I always thought, singularly clumsy. Although Denys was a large man, his head seemed to appear just above the steering wheel. We were taken for a joy ride. The Rolls moved off in a deliberate way, like an express train, making clanking noises.

Twenty-Eight

Denys was now preparing for a Christmas jaunt to Derbyshire. He and his brother had no particular regard for each other. His brother had expressed extreme disapproval of that folly, Chiddingstone Castle. Denys had been equally disapproving of his sister-in-law, whom he regarded as an unworthy match. This did not endear him to the lady, particularly in view of his own amatory adventures.

Nevertheless, Denys considered that it was proper for every family to be reunited at Christmas; there was also the unspoken assumption on Denys' part that it was his father's house, so he had, as it were, a patrial right to be there. Besides, he was looking forward to the opportunity of revisiting old friends and haunts.

He assembled a suitable stock of festive offerings, including a hamper from Fortnum's which he could in no way afford. It was indeed the return of the prodigal brother.

He planned to set off a few days before Christmas, leaving Chiddingstone early so as to arrive in Crich early in the evening.

We thought of him setting out, and of his probable progress during the day, but we did not expect to hear anything from him as his brother was not on the telephone – on principle, although what principle I do not know.

However, two days later, Ruth received a letter from him. It begun – as all unexpected communications (written and verbal) from him were to do, he knew they struck terror into our hearts – "There is nothing to worry about ... the car is all right really. Sanderson and Holmes can easily put it right."

He then explained what had happened. He was somewhere north of Leicester when he noticed that the car was not pulling as it should. But instead of getting out and looking under the bonnet – or even at the instrument panel, which would have told him a lot – he just put his foot down. The car managed to stumble on as far as Derby. Denys knew well the location of the famous Rolls Royce repairers. He limped into their forecourt and called for help. A mechanic tried to drive it round to the repair shop. It would not budge. He opened the bonnet. The engine had so over-heated that the engine head (being aluminium) had melted and become welded to the cylinder block.

Denys had notched up another first in the Guiness Book Records: the only person to have both frozen and melted a Rolls Royce engine.

He did not arrive in Crich until midnight. His brother had gone to bed, but his sister-in-law was sitting up for him wearily.

The trouble had been caused by the fine comb of the Rolls radiator, which gets blocked easily. The dealer should have checked it. As Denys said when he wrote to Mr Palmer, "You have sold me a pup."

There was nothing for it but to buy a new engine. But, as Denys said, fortunately Sanderson and Holmes happened to have a reconditioned one, and they could fit it at once. Total cost of all repairs would be £600 – almost as much as he had paid for the car. No allowance for the old engine of course: that was only fit for scrap. But, Denys pointed out consolingly, the car would be good as new – and Mr Palmer should make a contribution. (Which Mr Palmer did, though not without some reflections on Denys' driving common sense.)

There was no choice. Ruth had to find the money somehow for the Rolls – it was the first of the perpetual financial setbacks she was to have with Chidd. The repairs would take about a fortnight. Denys would have a couple of jolly weeks roaming Derbyshire, and his sister-in-law would just have to put up with him.

Twenty-Nine

In the meantime, the appalling winter of 1963 was setting in. Ruth, knowing that Denys' return was imminent, went down to see how things were at Chiddingstone She found the Waters stoically preparing for the long siege.

She drove away by Vexour Bridge. As she edged her way along the lane – much narrower than it is now – the snow laden hedgerow trees dipped over her head. She must have been almost the last to pass that way for many weeks.

When she got back to town she sent a telegram to Denys, telling him that the Castle was inaccessible, and advising him to postpone his return until he got the all clear from her.

The following Sunday morning we were preparing for morning coffee when the front door bell rang. Who could it be? We always had this little debate when there was an unexpected caller. It was annoying to go down three flights of stairs only to find a Jehovah's Witness. I went down – Ruth followed out of curiosity.

I opened the door. In bounced Denys and embraced us both heartily. "What are you doing here?" cried Ruth. "Didn't you get my telegram?"

"Yes, but I was thrown out."

The resplendent Rolls was parked outside, now in the best of health, said Denys. We felt it certainly gave tone to Mr Eldridge's residence. Denys came upstairs to join us for coffee and tell us his adventures.

He had been out when the telegram arrived. When he returned, it was lying on the sideboard, his sister-in-law looking stony. "You've read what Miss Eldridge says," Denys had said. Yes, she had, and took a poor view of it. A neighbour had just returned from London and said the roads were perfectly passable. She made it quite clear that Crich hospitality was at an end.

Next morning he prepared for an early departure. His sister-in-law's father, a genial old man, offered to help load the car. He was taking back some family things inherited from his mother, besides some little purchases he had made. "Let him do it himself," said Janet, who was probably none too pleased to see the heirlooms go. One or two got dropped in the snow and were broken. He made St Albans and put up at a hotel without water.

What was to be done about Denys? There was really only one answer. He would stay with us until the weather cleared. Which it did about ten weeks later.

We arranged a temporary home for the Rolls at Selfridge's garage. We got out the little camp bed – which was much too small for Denys and eventually collapsed under the strain – and the draught screen. This bulged rather with all his possessions behind it, and as he acquired more things it advanced further.

Thirty

It says a great deal for Denys' good nature and good manners that he was never an unwanted guest. He never presumed on familiarity, nor was he too formal. He was never a bore. His little bed was made and his corner tidied first thing every morning. He just became one of the family – a relationship which lasted all his life. And no doubt at this stage it was particularly fortunate he could come home and recount his doings to sympathetic listeners, and relearn the regular timetable of family life.

Denys' daily life followed a regular routine. He left 84 at nine o'clock returning a little after five. He spent the whole day wandering around London, north, south, east and west, visiting old haunts – it was really the best thing that could have happened, for he found his own way back into life. When he got back he settled down until dinner-time chatting to Mama, who was really quite fond of him. He knew this, and it made him all the more communicative and ready to take rebukes from her.

He had this characteristic: that if he knew people liked him he behaved very well with them – so they liked him all the better, and could not understand that any should find him difficult. To those who were antagonistic he behaved impishly. They reacted against each other until Denys did become very awkward indeed.

Sometimes we went out in the evenings, but the weather did not encourage this – though the streets were never impassable. Sometimes it was hard to realise how bad things were outside London.

At weekends we had many jaunts – mostly to museums. We learned a great deal from Denys. He imparted knowledge very easily and with great enthusiasm.

One fascinating place he introduced us to was Austin's of Peckham. They were second-hand dealers, and at that time had two enormous warehouses. They had everything – furniture, carpets, pictures, china, glass ... from ten shillings upwards. They did have some very good antiques – just thrown in with the rest, it was a real treasure hunt.

The first time we went I was lucky. I dived into a mass of grotty picture frames and came out with a most beautiful watercolour, one of the loveliest I have ever seen – a view of the coast of Asia Minor, unsigned, and obviously by a fine artist. Denys was impressed, and after that regarded us as knowledgeable collectors. He told me where to get it remounted and framed. The picture cost me £4.10s and the framing not much more.

Austin's are I think still there, but the last time I visited them all was neatly arranged – and astutely valued.

One afternoon Ruth and I returned to find Denys had fetched his inro collection from Sotheby's. It had been lying there under threat of sale. The lovely little things – all 220 of them – were spread out over the sitting room, and Denys and Mama were busy polishing them. Denys said the best thing was natural oil, and he used to sit rubbing them on the side of his nose, which did bring them up very well.

Some of the inro had lost their cords. There was an old-fashioned shop in Holborn where you could buy all sorts of narrow coloured cord, ideal for inro. I got a good supply and we spent many evenings stringing them up. Some were quite hard to do, and I was particularly proud of my success in dealing with a little rat which Denys said was an impossibility. It was one of those which was stolen. I grieve especially for the loss of those inro, they were such intimate friends.

Eventually, towards the end of March, Waters announced that the drive to the Castle was clear at last, so we all went down together. The Castle was awash with a plethora of burst pipes. One of the troubles was that in the past Mankelow had simply knocked any holes together with a hammer. Another awful expense. We had to find a real plumber.

We thought that Denys, having found his feet, might wish to be independent of us. But no; we received a note during the week, ending with the subscription: CU SAT. It was to become a regular weekly communication. Our task had not yet ended.

Thirty-One

We had to work very hard. When the weather was bad we worked in the house – painting, decorating, relining the cases, anything at all. When it was fine we worked in the grounds.

Denys appointed me his Head Gardener. There was actually a part-time under-gardener – George, a retired roadman. His hobby was growing vegetables, but he did not know about garden plants, and would do unrequested things, like pruning little trees as if they were rose bushes. But he was good natured and turned a good sod.

Then we always had missions to perform in town – such as finding a cheap supplier of picture postcards. I was recommended to a very inexpensive place off St Martin's Lane. One of those independent small businesses which lurked about in lost corners of London, and which Development has now swept away.

Their speciality was reproducing pictures of theatrical celebrities. The manageress became very interested in Chiddingstone, and always produced rush orders on time. Unfortunately they tended not to wash the prints sufficiently, so that they faded very quickly. They always replaced them willingly; but we thought guiltily of the unlucky visitors who had invested in them. I suppose their ephemeral nature did not matter in the fickle show business. After Denys' death we put them away, but a zealous custodian put them on sale again. There may still be some around. After thirty years they can be regarded as safe.

Sir Phillip and Lady Babbington were frequently about the house. The Air Vice Marshall liked to mend the clocks, unsuccessfully ... they lived in the village and loved the Castle.

One constant friend – and his open support must have saved Denys from any social ostracism, was Lord Astor. He obviously liked Denys, and was a big enough man to do as he pleased. An embarrassing moment for Denys arose when Lord Astor invited him to one of his shoots – he still preserved and the Queen was a frequent visitor. (We passed her once in the lane at the back of the Castle, going into a field with a party.) There would have been much difficulty about getting a licence for a gun, but much, much worse from the social point of view – Denys did not know how to handle one.

After much thought he composed a regretful letter of refusal, saying, "My shooting days are over." After he had despatched the letter he realised the funny side of what he had said. He had a good laugh – and thought probably Lord Astor would too.

The Waters had planned to retire finally after about two years, and towards the end of 1963 the brother-in-law announced that he had found a suitable pair of Victorian cottages near Glastonbury – unmodernised, but only £200. It was too good an opportunity to miss, and to their regret and ours, they decided to go.

The sister and brother-in-law came down to visit Chidd. Neville was a very superior person. He made it quite clear that Chidd was a dump, which embarrassed his wife, and also that he had married beneath him, which his wife did not mind as she was used to it. We wondered apprehensively how the arrangement would work. Waters did not like Neville, who would obviously sit around doing nothing and expect the Waters to do all the work. The project was breaking down even before it started. But the Waters decided it was better to get on with it.

They left Chiddingstone with a bath and wash basin (remnants of the School's ablutions). Denys presented them with a mezzotint of Charles I on horseback. I hope the Waters realised how difficult it must have been for him to part with it.

The Waters spent many happy years at Glastonbury. They eventually got their cottage modernised, and Mr Waters got a job as curator of the old Stone House in Glastonbury (said to be the oldest town house in England). He enjoyed it and they were very lucky to have him.

Their successors were an ill-assorted couple. She was so self-effacing that I cannot remember her – perhaps worn down by a domineering husband who was what is called a sergeant major type, though he had not been in the army. In spite of coarse management he had a puritanical outlook. We saw this for ourselves one Sunday afternoon.

It was the topless era, and the young woman accompanying a fisherman had stripped off and was lying in the grass semi-starkers – rather picturesque, like Manet's Picnic. When he spied her, he turned purple. He tore down to the lake, flailing his arms and yelling Biblical imprecations, and saw that decency was observed. Perhaps just as well, for visitors were coming and sunbathing right in front of the Castle.

It may be wondered how the Castle could be run with just one couple. It was difficult, but at that time there was no shop or tearoom to cope with. Denys did play a full part though he never revealed to visitors who he was; and at weekends we all went down. Our parents were very good at keeping a watch on visitors in the rooms. (My mother also insisted on tidying up Denys' kitchen. "Just a grub," she said with resignation.) Also it was possible to get young people from the village to help with admission of visitors. They were generally very efficient.

But it was always a chore replacing the resident couple. It involved a lot of advertising, much correspondence – which fell to my lot, I was not a bad typist by this time – and interviewing. The sergeant major lasted for about eighteen months, and was succeeded by Captain and Mrs Bell, a really nice couple. Captain Bell had suffered a bad war wound which had never healed and thought he might be able to manage the job at Chiddingstone.

The Bells did not stay very long. Captain Bell found that with his disability the work was too much for him, and he was offered a flat in a settlement for disabled officers. Ruth was rather cross with Denys, because she thought Bell might have stayed if he had not been pressed so hard – having to go out on the roof for instance. So she told him she would have to advertise in *The Lady*, sort out the replies and let him do the interviewing and engagement. One likely pair were selected, so Denys duly got in touch with them and interviewed them.

He telephoned Ruth in some dismay. The lady – a true iron lady – had turned out to be the dominant partner, and when he sked at the end of the interview if they would like to be considered the "Iron Lady" said she accepted the post, asked for a date for commencement and said that of course the flat would have to be altered. Indeed she seemed to want it re-orientated. In vain did Denys protest that he was not actually offering the post and murmured about other applicants. What was he to do? He could not bear the thought of life with the "Iron Lady". "Ask her to come on Saturday and I will see her," said Ruth.

The Lady had to be fetched from Edenbridge Station. On the way back Ruth said she believed she wanted some alterations done to the flat, so at Chidd they both went round it, she talking and Ruth silent. At the end of it all Ruth said it was impossible to do any of the things she required – obviously she would not be happy with things as they were – negotiations at an end. The lady withdrew some of her requirements. No, no, said Ruth, ushering her into the car, she could see that Chidd would not suit her at all. By the time they reached Edenbridge, the lady was ready to take the flat as it was. "No," said Ruth firmly. She could see it would not really suit her.

One of the other applicants was a Master Mariner. He seemed a quiet sort of man – his wife even quieter. Such an experienced sailor would, we thought, have some ideal qualifications – used to heights ("Are you good on roofs?" as Denys used to ask applicants) used to water and resourceful. We were mistaken.

At Christmas Denys went as usual to Crich. Just after Christmas the mariner rang late in the evening. There had been a frost, then a thaw. One of the pipes had burst and it was fed by a continuous flow of water from the great tank in the north tower. What was he to do? Turn the water off at the stop cock, said Ruth. He seemed reluctant. He did not relish climbing up the north tower. Another call. He could not find the stop cock. Try and get the plumber, said Ruth. Plumber not available. The calls went on during the night, reporting the onward and downward progress of the water. Once we got a crossed line, and could hear him talking to the night shift operator. The telephone was still human then. "They've left me," he wailed. "... all alone here, and the water pouring in."

"Too bad old chap," the operator sympathised. "Sorry I can't help you."

Ruth had just dropped off to sleep at 5 o'clock when the telephone rang for the last time. "The water has stopped coming in now." But it had reached the ground floor, via the Japanese room ceiling – part of which collapsed. Unexpectedly, he got another job – with a Greek shipping line. He was going to sea again, but he assured us, he would not have to do anything. Maritime regulations required that they have someone with a master's certificate on board. His mere presence was sufficient.

So we started on another search. In the meantime we managed with volunteers. Denys had a few friends who helped with the care of the collections. The more assiduous of these was Tom Gregory, whom Denys always referred to ceremoniously as "Mr Gregory." He came every Monday. Denys prepared a careful collation for him, of which the staple item was a David Greig pork pie – Mr Gregory's favourite. "It goes down very well," said Denys gravely.

Mr Gregory was a civil engineer, his speciality being swing bridges – he was in partnership with his brother. He was also an expert on metals and armour, which he collected. He advised on the Black Prince's reconstructed helmet in Canterbury Cathedral. The authorities did not know what sort of iron it was made of. He told them, and that the only place they might find it now would be in Sweden. The Swedes produced it and gave it free. (The original helmet is too frail to be displayed.)

In the end we got one of the best couples Chidd has had – the Hatchers. Reg was a retired bank official. He should have been a manager, but he did not like settling anywhere. He was tall, thin and dignified – he was rather like Denys, a conventional appearance concealed Bohemian inclinations. His wife Marjory was tall, stout and jolly with an equal wanderlust – they were a well-matched pair, for neither could bear owning property. They always rented. I remember meeting them in the courtyard garden. Marjory suddenly laughed and said, "We'll come!"

They got on well with Denys, and any awkward moments resolved themselves. After they had left, Marjory told me of one instance. It had been a particularly busy and troublesome Sunday afternoon. They were just locking up when a party of intruders were seen going over the bridge. "Just run and show them off." Marjory said she could see that Reg did not like this peremptory order from Denys. Nevertheless he went. Denys finished doing the ticket book and went upstairs to his quarters.

As the Hatchers went upstairs back to their flat, there was Denys standing at the door with his silver tray set out with sherry and his lovely antique glasses. "We're all tired and need some refreshment." So they had a little carousal.

After about 18 months the Hatchers decided to leave, to everyone's regret. Marjory was having trouble with her legs, and the Penshurst doctor advised that Chidd involved too much walking. She said indignantly that he seemed to have something against Chidd for he said, "You don't want to work there!"

They went to live at Littlehampton, where Marjory's legs were treated successfully at the local hospital. She was very bitter about the doctor's advice, for she said he had driven them from Chidd where they were having the time of their life. It is true her legs let her down in the end, for she was bedridden for the last two years of her life. But that was thirteen years or so later.

They were succeeded by a lady with a career in the police. She told us that she was known as the Duchess, because of her impressive deportment. I do not remember anything about her husband – he was not in the ducal class. She brought her pets with her – two lovely golden pheasants. They wandered about the grounds for a few weeks giving great tone to the place. Then they disappeared – whether into Lord Astor's bag or on a frolic of their own we never knew.

Then the Duchess got restless, like her pheasants, and departed ...

Thirty-Two

After the uneasy period things settled a little and the custodians became more stable, but it was Tom Gregory who gave Denys the firmest support. The occupant of the bungalow decided to go, and Tom and Mrs Gregory came to live there and helped us as custodians. Tom was invaluable, because with his technical knowledge he did all sorts of practical work about the Castle.

It was a lonely life for Denys, but he was living in the midst of the treasures he loved and, as he once said to my father with delight, he had never been so free of financial worry in his life. He did not always take his share in keeping Chiddingstone solvent, and his first venture into the world of major antiques gave Ruth a foretaste of what she would have to contend with.

He kept up his interest in the collecting world. He subscribed to Christie's and Sotheby's catalogues. We used to have interesting discussions about them. Not long after his return to Chidd he pointed out an interesting lot in a forthcoming Sotheby sale – a little cream coloured Longton Hall mug, decorated with a black transfer print – but not of the usual popular hero, the King of Prussia (Frederick the

Great) but of Prince Charles Edward. Now this was interesting indeed. The printing was usually done at Liverpool – but no one has ever discovered what factory was bold enough to celebrate Bonnie Prince Charlie. It could have been a capital offence. Denys knew I haunted all the porcelain sales, so he asked me to look at the mug, tell him what I thought of it, and ask the likely sale price. So I did.

I told him I thought it rather an undistinguished bit of potting. Estimated price £80. Entirely due to its extreme rarity. You could get a beautiful Worcester blue scale mug for half the price. I told him he need not regret the mug – he was not missing an aesthetic treat. But I had forgotten – that was not what interested him.

When I studied the results of the sale I got a shock. The mug had been knocked down to Denys Bower for £120. Ruth was furious. All her scheming and scrimping had gone for nothing. So she simply wrote and told him that since he was not prepared to take her advice she could no longer act for him. He must find another solicitor. She would have said a lot more but my father restrained her.

There was silence from Denys for several days. Then later in the week, just before lunchtime, her office door opened silently. She looked up in surprise. The top of a head appeared round the door, then more of it – then Denys. "Ex-convict invites ex-solicitor out to lunch," he said. She nearly fell under her desk with laughing. He laughed too, and they went out to lunch together. After that she said she would not worry about controlling his spending. If necessary he would just have to sell something.

Why did Ruth take on so much trouble and worry? In the first place, there was Denys himself. It was obvious he could not survive on his own. To abandon him would be rather like letting go of a drowning man whom you had just rescued, and leaving him to drown. Besides, he was a genius in his way. He was modest about this; always said he was not creative, not original. But he was truly an artist, and like many artists he needed an impresario.

Then there was the Castle and its collections. The house was part of English history and architecture, and its contents were a marvellous assemblage. They MUST survive at all costs. The truth was we were in thrall, both of us, to the place. In some ways we were more concerned about it than Denys, for we saw that plans must be made for its future, whereas he lived from day to day as he had always done. So she persevered.

But Denys did enjoy life, and if he could not have the excitement of Christie's and Sotheby's there were local sales where you could pick up all sorts of exciting lots, including useful pieces of domestic equipment.

The Castle at thus period had not been done up at all, apart from our personal efforts at patching. It was all painted cream, and had no curtains of any sort. Denys had once acquired some red silk ones for the White Rose Room at a Penshurst sale, but they had fallen to bits. They were too short anyway. Mrs Veall however, kept the place spotless.

There was not much domestic equipment for her to work with, and we thought that the wooden floor of the Great Hall required an electric rubber. But the 'frotteur', so universal in France, had not yet arrived in England. One weekend Denys told us triumphantly that he had something to show us. He took us into the Great Hall and there was a 'frotteur'. He had found it at some local sale. He demonstrated it for us. It was a powerful machine and careered off down the Hall with him after it – holding it with one hand, and waving the other elegantly in the air, and pirouetting like a ballet dancer. He was so graceful he could do that kind of thing without looking awkward.

Thirty-Three

He did, though, still have his ventures into the antiques world, though he was careful to consult Ruth about the economics of it first. One day he telephoned her to say he had had a find at Austin's – a large Japanese Imari vessel set in 18th century ormulu of the finest quality.

Denys was quite sure of its authenticity and artistic quality, and he thought that in the saleroom it should fetch at least £400. It would be a good way of raising a bit of money. Ruth respected his artistic and saleroom judgement, so she agreed he should go ahead with the purchase.

Sotheby's expert had other views however – thought it might make £250, more likely £200. Denys left the bowl with them disconsolately, wondering how to set the reserve. It looked as though very little profit would be made on the deal – hardly worth the trouble.

But a little later, Denys was elated by better news. One of Sotheby's younger valuers said it was the most remarkable bowl he had ever seen; should fetch at least £700, and the reserve should not be less than £400. "These younger ones are much more with it," remarked Denys. So all was arranged – reserve of £400.

But the evening before the sale Denys telephoned again. The young expert must have been rebuked by his superior. For he had telephoned again to say he had been a little too hopeful. Bowl not worth more than £400.

Denys was in a dilemma. He was quite sure of his judgement; someone ought to bid it up, he said, but unfortunately he could not go to the sale. All right Denys, I volunteered rashly. "I have a day's holiday tomorrow – I can easily look in at Sotheby's – it's at the beginning of the sale, won't take me half an hour." Denys was grateful beyond words.

"I won't let it go for less than £700."

"Sure?"

"Quite sure."

This meant that if I had to bid I should get in my last bid at £675. Quite a tricky business. I remembered the silver coffee pot.

So next morning I dressed carefully, looking I hoped like a person who could afford what she fancied, and went along to Sotheby's. It was a swagger sale, with the room set out with little gilt rout chairs, so that the rich could take their ease. I got a seat near the front. On one side was a Frenchman, and when the bidding began he joined in. Very encouraging, this was something that should appeal to the French collector. I was a little uneasy that the bowl should come so early on in the sale. One does not have time to get the feel of the room – whether it is going to be a good or a bad day; and those who are unsuccessful early may feel doubly tempted later on – especially private buyers.

At any rate, the bidding got off well, I had to nudge it at £400, then away it went. I was feeling happy when it stopped dead at £600 with my Frenchman. "625" I came in.

"650," the Frenchman and I were alone in the chase now. You can't pause for deliberation at an auction.

"£675," – my last bid, and I was left with the vase.

At the door of the saleroom I met Mama, who had come along to see the fun. Her face said: You idiot. But she confined herself to remarking, had I not noticed that the Frenchman's last bid was very reluctant. "I was told to bid to £700 and I did."

"But Denys needs the money," said Mama. She was dead right of course. We walked home in antagonistic silence.

Papa backed me. "Business arrangement – of course you had to do as instructed."

Denys was philosophical when I telephoned him. A pity, but it was the right thing to do. He would put it up again after a decent lapse of time. In the meantime he asked if we would mind having it on our sideboard (as it was a rather large and inconvenient object to transport to Chidd) – where it looked noble but unhappy – just longing to be back at Versailles.

In due course it returned to Sotheby's, and this time it romped away to £1200 without any prompting. Frank Davis illustrated it in his 'Sales Week' page in *Country Life*. Very fine if you like that sort of thing, he said; he did not. Neither did Denys.

Thirty-Four

Denys' periodic sallies into the saleroom were a help in keeping Chidd going.

Sometimes the contents of the house showed unexpected capabilities. There was the marble bas-relief, a massive roundel hanging in the Great Hall – a rather unpleasant scene of the martyrdom of St Someone or other, one of those Italian Renaissance experiences which one cannot help feeling were an excuse for a respectable bit of sadism. Denys read somewhere that the terracotta model for it had been identified – but where, the experts wondered, was the carving itself? Denys was very happy to produce it for them – he had never liked it. It made its mark in the saleroom.

Local purchases sometimes had unexpected results. He had bought a lot containing an Egyptian wooden pillow or headrest, which cost him £80, more than he could afford. Amongst the crocks that went with it was a little bottle in the style of 17th century Lambeth, with round body and long slim neck, cream coloured and with the date 1675 painted in blue. It was only 5"-6" high – the only known Lambeth bottles being twice the size. "Must be a modern imitation," said Denys. However. After living with the little trifle for a week he was not so sure. After a fortnight he was sure he had a winner, and took it to Sotheby's. They were incredulous at first, but a test confirmed its antiquity. It helped considerably with the funds. A year or two ago I read an article in *Country Life* which referred to this 'unique' vessel – it must have been the same one.

An even greater scoop was at a local jumble sale. There Denys acquired a 17th century etching. It depicted a stout, very unprepossessing young woman, very much over-dressed. One could see why it had ended up at a jumble sale. "The Jewish Bride," said Denys. "One of Rembrandt's lesser known etchings – and a good impression too." I believe it raised about £2000.

The last incident illustrates one of the reasons for Denys' success in collecting – the failure of the general public to recognise fine quality if they do not like the subject matter of a work of art. Ruth hoped that some of this money might go towards the reparation of the roof. But Denys was cagey about how he disposed of it. Perhaps he thought that these little extras being acquired by his own wits and not a regular part of the Castle income could legitimately be used for his own little escapades. We learned after his death that he had been investing quite heavily in Stuart manuscripts.

Thirty-Five

As Ruth had recognised from the first, visitor's entrance fees were far too irregular as a source of income. Her remedy, the flats, were long delayed in completion – a constant problem with building work at Chiddingstone. When they were ready for letting, we were also unfortunate in our first tenants. The lot of landlords is not so easy as some people might imagine.

The larger flat was let to a tenant who was pleasant, but always behind with his rent. He had a garage which went bust – thus explaining the difficulties. It was taken by Lady Babbington after his departure – Sir Philip having died. The smaller flat was taken by a nice young couple from Rhodesia – the husband was a student on a government grant. But when the Rhodesian government stopped student grants, they could not pay the rent either. They had some rather good Oriental rugs which they sold to pay their debts and departed – we were very sorry for them.

The coach house was free after the tenant left. It was taken by Grant Uden and his wife. Grant Uden was a distinguished inspector of schools, an author, who took early retirement to devote himself to writing. He and Denys became great friends. He loved the library, where he often worked. Mrs Uden was also devoted to the collection and preservation of antiques, to which she was quite ready to sacrifice her own convenience. Once, when they were on holiday in Suffolk, they found a dough trough on their very first day. It was too fragile to entrust to a carrier, so Mrs Uden just bundled up all her clothes, sent them back to the Castle by post and the dough bin travelled in the car.

I well remember my first meeting with them. It was a Saturday, and as we drove up the drive I noticed the Udens, just finishing planting a border outside the cottage. They were keen gardeners, and had brought their own plants with them. We went round to the south front, where I found George just finishing off his morning's work. I asked him to go and dig up a rose and pyracantha I had unwisely planted against the fence bordering the little drive from the north front to the garages.

Sometime later he wheeled a loaded barrow to the south entrance, waved to me and disappeared. I did not examine the contents of the barrow until after lunch. My treasures were constantly being run over in their old position and I had to find them a new home. I was astonished at the exotic contents of the barrow – plants I had never seen. Where on earth had George found them? A dreadful thought seized me. I ran to the north front. Yes, as I feared. George had presented me with the contents of the Uden's newly planted border. I hardly knew what to say. The Udens took it in a very sporting way, and insisted on replanting the border themselves.

The Udens left the cottage in 1968 and went down to the West Country. Denys kept in touch with them, and it was Grant Uden who made a valuation of the library after Denys' death. He carefully removed the books which he said were not worth much and left them stacked so we could get rid of them. We looked at them, thought they were very interesting, and put them back.

Thirty-Six

It was at this time – October 1965 – Chidd suffered its first devastating theft. The roof, as ever, was giving trouble, and some essential repairs had to be carried out. Nothing is more dangerous to security than to allow strangers to get a knowledge of the roof. Denys suggested, very sensibly, that we should employ an old established firm with presumably a long established, reliable staff. What we did not know was that they contracted out the roofing.

Only those with an intimate knowledge of the building could have found their way into the Japanese room; only those with private access could have left various windows and doors ready prepared for the intruders. There was no alarm system then – country house burglaries were an extreme rarity.

They took the whole of the Netsuke collection, which was a very fine one, and twenty-five swords. There must have been two or three men, for the swords would be a heavy load. They took one of the lacquer sword rests, but discarded it on a pile of rubbish near the orangery. It was not noticed, and was put on the bonfire. The charred remains still showed traces of the lovely black and gold lacquer.

The thieves easily escaped. It was a wild, rainy night, and

no one heard them. Denys discovered the loss when he was making his morning rounds. It was Saturday, and we heard about it as soon as we arrived – the first of the awful shocks to which we were to become accustomed.

Denys was philosophical. No hope for the Netsuke, he said: they would already be out of the country. But the swords were more difficult to dispose of. And for two years Denys watched for them, at every sword sale – every antique shop he passed. At last he tracked one of them down. It was a clue to the whole crime – but that is a saga in itself. All the swords came back home eventually – two of them after his death.

Thirty-Seven

In 1965 my father had a very serious illness and decided to retire. For some years we had been looking for a country cottage in a desultory sort of way. When the coach house became vacant, Denys pressed us to take it, but we wanted a place of our own. We didn't relish the prospect of our services being entirely commandeered by the Castle – though they were anyway, probably a residence there would hardly have made any difference. Denys was very helpful in looking out for suitable places, and inspecting them with us.

We found the cottage at Ticehurst at the end of 1965, but there were delays and my parents did not move in until July 1966. After that we did not go so regularly to Chidd on Saturdays. I gave up the garden at Chidd because we had one at Ticehurst to cope with, and only supervised the planting. Denys at once engaged a local man to do the digging. I felt a bit cheesed. He might have done that earlier, instead of expecting us to slave away at it, just to save Chidd a little money.

Denys came over to dinner at Ticehurst every Saturday, and told us all his doings, and brought over any little acquisitions for inspection. Ruth and I went over to Chidd on Sunday mornings to do odd jobs.

My father had been in frail health for some time but was quite active. But one Saturday when Denys came as usual for dinner, he could not leave his room. He sent Denys a message that he looked forward to seeing him the following week. Within a few days he was dead.

Denys was shattered by this loss for he was devoted to my father. When I telephoned him with the news there was a short silence. Then he said, "It is the end of an era."

He offered to do everything he could to help us, and indeed his help was invaluable, for the clutch of our car gave trouble and it was out of action for several days. Denys took us anywhere we wanted.

My father was to be buried with my mother's parents in a cemetery at Maidenhead. Her people had no permanent connection with the place – her parents happened to be living with one of their sons who was in practice there, at the time they died.

It was unfortunate that just at this point the weather turned snowy. Ruth and I could get to Maidenhead by car – my mother did not come – for the main road was clear. But minor cross-country roads were very dangerous, so we asked friends not to come – my father would not have wished to expose them to risk.

We pulled up at a small pub just outside Maidenhead for a snack – and were astonished to see Denys' Rolls in the car park. We found him inside enjoying a sandwich. He must have had an appalling journey, but he said he felt he must come. He was not a self-confident driver, so his determination showed great courage on his part.

Thirty-Eight

During the Spring of 1970 we put in a lot of hard work at Chidd. We felt it was really time to do up the White Rose Drawing Room, which looked bleak indeed, with its cream-coloured walls (rather dirty by this time) and makeshift ceiling. During the War, there was a little fire in the drawing room, and what with the flames and the water used to douse them the whole plaster ceiling fell down. A builder who was a voluntary member of the fire brigade described it to us – it seems to have been an attractive affair, with plaster Adam-style decoration. The cornice had gone too. It had been replaced with sections of plaster board, with no attempt to hide the joints – serviceable but ugly. What could be done about it?

Complete replastering would have been prohibitively expensive – even plain plaster without decorative details. So it was decided to cover the joints with decorative fibre plaster 'beams' to make it look like a coffered ceiling and put a cornice in the same material. They were supplied by a firm in Fulham which specialises in reproduction Georgian details – over the years they have been collecting genuine Georgian plasterwork from old houses, from which they have made casts. (They supplied the moulding for the Goodhugh room.) Tom Gregory and Mr Medhurst put it up between them when the tower scaffold was bought. Tom Gregory was the engineer, for Medhurst had a little difficulty in getting the plasterwork to meet exactly. In some places it does not, but we said it looked realistic, like ancient wear.

Tom and Denys were particularly careful about the chandelier – a lovely Waterford model, finer than the present one. They both lowered it on a rope, no workman could be trusted with it. When they came to placing it back in position something went wrong however. It was never quite clear what happened, but one of them let go at the wrong moment, and the chandelier came crashing to the ground. It was not only the fall that destroyed it, but the heavy armature crushed the fragile drops. Denys was stoical about it, as he usually was about disasters. He collected all the undamaged drops and traded them in for payment for another chandelier, which he got from an antique dealer in Westerham.

Ruth and I did our bit doing the dado. We got a very nice flock wallpaper from Coles and spent every Sunday morning for weeks putting it up.

I have mentioned our decorator Mr Medhurst. He was a fine old craftsman, a native of Chiddingstone – Medhurst is an old local name. As a boy his first job was working at the Castle in 1893, on Maples modernisation. He lived at Highfield, a timber framed medieval house in the woods of Hill Hoath, said to have been used one time as a dower house, by the Streatfeilds. Denys came upon it soon after he settled at Chiddingstone – he was taking an evening walk and suddenly saw the old mansion looming out of the trees, like something out of a fairy tale.

Mr Medhurst married when he was seventy, and had several children (one of them is Pam, who looks after the Castle so beautifully). The local authority, perhaps alarmed at the prospect of young children growing up in such primitive conditions condemned the house as unfit for habitation and rehoused the family in a council house. The decaying house was a target for squatters; it was on Lord Astor's land and he pulled it down. There was some local antiquarian protest – Medhurst was very aggrieved. He told Denys it contained some fine panelling and carving – all put on the bonfire.

Mr Medhurst was now in his eighties, doing odd decorating jobs. He told Denys when he first did work at the Castle, that he did not like these jobs. He got chivvied for being slow. Denys, recognising a good craftsman said he could have as much work as he wanted at the Castle, and go his own pace in peace and quiet. The paintwork in the drawing room is an example of his skill.

Denys was so pleased with the general effect that he had the small Stuart room done the same way. The Great Staircase had already been repainted. Rampant dry rot had appeared in the woodwork above the great window, and Rentokil were called in to treat it. The ceiling was done at the same time. A special gilder was brought in to do the gold leaf, and it was fascinating to watch how he flicked it on. The gilding has not been touched since – that is the advantage of real gold – expensive in the first place, but it lasts indefinitely.

For the colour of the walls Denys consulted an architect who specialised in Georgian interiors. He advised Chinese yellow – i.e. the colour of the enamel on the cloisonné work in the Buddhist room. One weekend when we called, the first section had been completed. It was a most unpleasant, ochreous yellow. "That is NOT Chinese yellow," we said. Oh yes it was, said Denys. The builder says so. "You know perfectly well it is not. Tell the builder to give you some sample patches." Finally Denys did admit that the colour was wrong, but he would do nothing about it. Strange, for he usually insisted on things being exactly right. He said the colour would tone down with time. But it never did. It got worse.

The staircase was done during the regime of the Hatchers. For months the scaffolding was up, so that they practically had to crawl up and down stairs, and I think this contributed to their decision to leave.

Thirty-Nine

Just at this time Denys got some unexpected assistance which he hoped would be permanent, thought in fact it lasted only a few months – a cousin, Susan, married to a colonel in the Regular Army. He had been seconded to the army of the Emirate of Abu Dhabi. It was a strange arrangement, one of the last remnants of our Imperial tradition. Abu Dhabi had been protected by the British Army, but the Emir decided he would prefer to organise his own forces. The colonel was to return home. But at the last minute the Emir decided he would retain the British officers in command.

Arrangements had already been made for the children, and his cousin Susan to return home, and it was decided not to alter this plan, especially as the Emir's intentions were still indefinite. So they agreed with Denys that Susan should have a flat at Chidd and help with visitors. The children would stay there when on holiday, and their father Derek, when he was on leave.

Denys was delighted. He said Derek was a very practical person who would be able to repair the Well Tower roof which was giving trouble. Some rooms were prepared for Susan in the attic. It was very primitive, but she was a charming and resourceful person used to emergencies.

It was during Susan's time that the Enterprise Neptune Ball was held at Chidd. Denys lent the grounds to the NT for a ball in aid of the scheme. It was a very smart affair – full evening dress – held in a marquee. Unfortunately there was a lack of liaison between the hirers of the grand piano and the hirers of the marquee. The marquee people appeared promptly on Sunday morning, removed the marquee, and left the grand piano standing in the middle of the south field. It rained. Denys did nothing about it, which horrified us. We reproached him. He was unrepentant – said it was nothing to do with him. Anyway, what could he have done? Putting a mackintosh over it would have been no use. The truth was, I'm afraid, that he had no particular affection for grand pianos. Otherwise he could at least have had it hauled into the south entrance.

The colonel did not repair the Well Tower roof, as Denys had hoped. In fact his plans changed entirely. The Emir had decided that he would after all retain English officers in command of his army, so Derek returned permanently to Abu Dhabi; and Susan went to Derbyshire to settle the children at school.

Forty

Early in 1971 Denys took his first holiday – a trip down the Adriatic to Turkey. A few days before he was due to leave he telephoned Ruth to say that he wished to make a will. It was a matter she had urged on him many times. Many years ago he had made a will leaving everything to his brother, but he had destroyed it when he was in prison. He knew that his brother disapproved of the Castle and would sell it once it was in his possession.

In response to Ruth's promptings, Denys' only response was to say he would leave it to her. Grateful clients not infrequently make this suggestion to their solicitor, and, as a good solicitor should, Ruth refused. Besides, she told Denys, she would at once make it over to the National Trust – far better that he should have the honour and glory of doing that. But, she pointed out, Denys would have to discuss the offer with them first, as usually acceptance was dependent on a massive endowment.

She did not suggest the alternative of setting up a private charitable trust with herself as Trustee. Such an awful possibility did not occur to her.

So when Denys at last announced his intention of making

a will she was immensely relieved. Who was to be the beneficiary, she asked. Why, the National Trust of course, he said. He had not discussed it with them. Although there was no endowment, he pointed out to Ruth that it paid its way – and most important, the Trust owned the village. It should be re-united with the Squire's house.

It was an unselfish gesture on his part, because he did not really like the National Trust. There had already been murmurings about acquiring some of the Castle grounds as a car park. Once in their possession, there would certainly be pressure on the Trust to make this a solution to the parking problem in the village. The will should be carefully framed, so as to put this out of their power.

There was the risk that the National Trust might accept the gift, keep the land they wanted, and sell off the house and all its contents., except for what they might select for other houses. So she framed the will carefully , leaving it to the Trust as Trustees with certain expressed wishes. "It is my particular wish that at no time shall any of the land lying between the lake and the village be made into a car park ... I have devoted my life to making these Collections and it is my wish that they shall be kept intact in their present setting so that future generations may enjoy them as I do now." Mere wishes expressed by a testator are not always mandatory, but in these circumstances they would be.

Ruth did not want to put off Denys by making difficulties. He was pleased with the will and signed it. He said he would consider it again when he had more time and could discuss it with the National Trust.

He sent Ruth a note from the airport, enclosing a receipt for a life insurance policy for £100,000 which he had taken out just before leaving. "That should keep Chidd going," he wrote.

He was not over enthusiastic about his holiday and in fact said very little about it. He had not taken a sufficiently warm overcoat, and had found it very cold going down the Adriatic. As for his will, he never did approach the National Trust, and always put off the question of altering it.

The trip had done his health no good. He had a bad cough which went on until March. It was a cold winter, and he used to sit all crouched over a little electric fire, looking, we thought, rather like a crumpled bird. But he never complained.

From about 1973 we saw Denys less frequently – no more than once a month. The price of petrol went up so substantially that the cost of even a short journey in the Rolls was astronomical, too much, we thought, to justify the visit. Ruth was particularly busy at the office – had a lot of work to bring home – so that we could not get over to Chidd so often. However, Denys had long weekly talks with Ruth, on Sunday, by telephone. She was responsible for the finances as ever.

Forty-One

We missed his weekly visits, and his amusing chatter. Difficult he may have been at times, but he had endearing little gestures, which melted one's heart when one was getting fed up of him – as when he solemnly invested Ruth with a Good Conduct Medal. It was a beautifully engraved silver medal awarded to a member of the Coastguard Service in the 1840's.

Life at Chidd was not always easy for him, although he showed a remarkable lack of bitterness, which must have been difficult, for he never knew when he might be taunted with his past. We heard of one such instance after he was dead – he had never told us of it.

The large field next to Anthony Wood's property – the one with the pond in it – had been for sale for some time. Wood did not buy it because he thought it too highly priced, but eventually it was taken by someone who put horses and a caravan in it. The caravan gradually became more permanent. The site had no planning permission for a permanent dwelling. The Local Authority refused it on the grounds that it would be an unsuitable development, and issued a demolition order. The owner appealed.

There was a great feeling in the village about the case.

Many felt that it was quite wrong for someone to get away with a fait accompli, and that what was done was a blot on the landscape. Denys was one of those who gave evidence against the owner; and he was, so our informant said, doing very well, when the owner's counsel interjected: "Surely you are not going to listen to the evidence of an ex-convict." He should of course have been reprimanded by the Inspector, and reported to the Bar Council. Denys, we were told, just crumpled up and said no more.

Forty-Two

Some two years later Denys achieved another of his ambitions: a visit to Egypt. As with his previous holiday, he did not say much about it on his return. He was disappointed with the Egyptian museums – the Tutankhamun exhibits were not nearly so well displayed as they had been in London. He had been badly attacked by mosquitoes, and the dirt of Egypt dismayed him. He said he was watching some women prepare bread, and he wondered why they were putting currents in it. On closer inspection, he realised they were flies.

Things at last seemed to be going fairly smoothly at Chidd. When the custodians decided to retire, Denys found their successors himself. This was a great relief. He told us soon after that the couple, the Vinsons, were the best he had ever had.

Denys' final adventure was his visit to Japan at the beginning of 1977. He sold some swords to raise the money for this. It was a high-pressure tour to inspect the ancient monuments of Japan. The swords sold very well. Denys was delighted, and in going through his expenses with Ruth thought he could treat himself to the best. Ruth queried the amount but let it go. He deserved some fun.

Before Christmas Denys went to Derbyshire – both for Christmas and his niece's wedding. His brother he found in very low health. Denys took a poor view of his expectation of life. Nevertheless it was his brother who was the survivor.

Denys returned from the holiday a shattered man. The long air journey and non-stop activities of the holiday had put too much strain on his lungs. He developed a bad cough which lasted all winter. He had enjoyed the holiday, and had used the opportunity to take his broken articulated centipede to Japan, the only place where it could be repaired. He had left it in the care of the (GB) ambassador who said he would get it repaired and send it back to England.

The Castle did quite well that year. Numbers were going up. At that time there were fewer popular excursions, and many visitors to Chidd came for want of something else to do. They were a very mixed bag, and some of them gave a lot of trouble – especially those who came on Bank Holidays. These fringe visitors can now find entertainment elsewhere.

We always had a little celebration on Denys' birthday – 2nd July. So we took over a birthday feast and some presents.

It was a beautiful day and Chidd was looking lovely, better than we had ever seen it. Denys was very pleased to see us. He enjoyed little family parties. Mrs Vinson had made Denys a cake, and he had thought of inviting them along. But, he said, he thought it would be nicer to keep it to the family.

We had our celebration in the panelled sitting room. Denys used this for visitors now his own sitting room was practically impassable. We went and looked at it. It had been such an attractive room when we had got it ready for him. At any rate, said Denys cheerfully, it would defeat any burglar. Where were his particular treasures? The coins and medals, Egyptian things, miniature – the coffee pot we had already used. Denys pointed them out. If you shifted them there was a dust free patch where they had been. He would know at once if they had been shifted, he said.

As we were saying goodbye at the east door, we stopped and looked round. Ruth said to Denys, that the place seemed to be succeeding at last. He must feel very proud of it. He nodded, but said he felt very tired. It was the first time we had ever heard him admit to being tired.

We were preparing to drive off when my mother called to Denys. He bent down at her window, and she said, "Denys, you must see a doctor." He laughed and pooh-poohed the idea. She persisted. Promise me you will see a doctor. Again he laughed.

As we drove away, my mother said, "He is a sick man." She was always right in her predictions. I turned and looked back at Denys standing at the corner of the Castle and waved. It was the last time I ever saw him.

Forty-Three

On Sunday 14th August Ruth was particularly busy with business work which she had brought down with her to Ticehurst. It was not until seven in the evening that she realised she had not had the usual morning call from Denys. Surprised and a little concerned – for it was a routine he never missed – she telephoned him.

A very faint and weary voice answered her. Denys had been very unwell that week. He awoke one night, he said, with a terrible pain in his chest. He managed to get up and crawl as far as the Vinson's flat to ask for help. They called the doctor, who was a stand-in. He was uncertain what the trouble was, but gave Denys some pills and sent him back to bed. The next day, Wednesday, he had another attack. Another doctor came. Vinson said he thought Denys should go into hospital, for there was no one to look after him properly. Vinson told the doctor he thought Denys was really ill, beyond anything he or Mrs Vinson could do for him. The doctor replied that Denys was not ill enough for hospital. If he wanted he could go into a private home – he could afford it. (Vinson, not Denys, told us this afterwards.)

On Friday Denys had another attack. Yet another doctor

came, who said it was cardiac asthma, and prescribed some more pills. These seemed to be working, for Denys said he felt much better. Ruth said he ought to have told her earlier, but he said he did not want to worry her, and intended to say nothing about it until he was quite better. He was already feeling much better, he said. Ruth wanted to call round that evening, on her way back to London. He assured her there was no need, and that he would be quite all right. His voice was by this time much stronger and he said goodbye, laughing.

Next morning she had a telephone call from Chidd soon after she arrived at the office. She was busy, and thinking it was Denys for one of his usual chats she said she would ring back. Half an hour later came another call – again she said she would ring back.

Finally another call: the telephone operator told her that the Castle was on the line with the message that Mr Bower had died suddenly that morning.

Stunned, Ruth took the call. There was only a brief discussion of the funeral arrangements, and, to reassure the Vinsons about the future of the Castle, she spoke of the contents of Denys' will, and said she was immediately informing the National Trust. Then she telephoned me – I was at home, having recently retired.

I suppose Denys' eternally youthful spirit had deluded one into thinking he was eternal too. The ominous events of the last week should have warned us. This was the end of the fantasy, the fairy story. It was as if it had been a dream, and – as happens with dreams – we had been rudely awakened before it finished.

Would the Trust take it and methodically put it to rights? They are very thorough and sound on restoration. But the trouble with the Castle was, to what state should it be restored? Denys' vision had been born dilapidated. Well that would be the Trust's problem. Ruth's immediate task was to break the news to them of their unexpected good fortune.

The news was of course a complete surprise to them, not to say a shock. They said they would have to get in touch with their chairnan, Lord Antrim. It was not until the afternoon that they were able to inform Ruth that they would meet her the next day at the Castle.

Next day I went down to Chidd with Ruth, mournful and a little apprehensive. The problems of settling the future of Chidd did however take our minds off our personal feelings to some extent.

While Ruth was talking with Lord Antrim I went round the flat. It was in a state of chaos. The kitchen was unspeakable, a midden. We had not been permitted to see it for some time, and my mother's ministrations had ceased long ago. I learned of another misfortune. Denys had had an accident with the Rolls. He had been going under a bridge where a lorry was parked. Other traffic was going past it and Denys followed. He had reckoned without the girth of the Rolls. One side of the body was badly torn, so that the car was unusable. He had not mentioned this to us, but it accounted for his evasiveness when we asked him over to Ticehurst. I suppose he had felt too ill and depressed to do anything about it, and had not liked to mention the expense to Ruth.

Forty-Four

Ruth joined me when Lord Antrim had departed. He had been courteous, but non-committal. When looking at the Castle he had remarked that twenty years previously that type of architecture had been little respected, but that opinion about it was changing. He said the Trust team of experts would be sent in to inspect the place, because they could not accept it without a thorough assessment. But he did not say that lack of endowment made its acceptance impossible.

The National Trust did send in their team: architects with their drawing boards, the garden expert, the parking specialist, the tea room advisor – they seemed endless.

At the same time the Chiddingstone saga rolled on. The funeral took place at Tunbridge Wells Crematorium. A few friends and relations were present. The popular press were not there, not even a local reporter. Denys Bower was no longer news. He had escaped his pursuers forever. They never got their interview – 'not now or ever,' as Ruth had once said.

Among the mourners were Denys' niece Rosemary, and her newly wed husband. A possible heiress, if the National Trust turned down the Castle? But she was not so impolite as to mention this.

The Trust experts were still working away when Vinson told us that a local committee had come to make an inspection. Who they were he did not know, but they seemed unfriendly and supercilious – not at all like Lord Antrim. Soon after their visit we were informed that the Trust would not be accepting the castle – there was no money, and looking after the collections was a matter they could not undertake. It was strange that they had sent no expert to examine the collections, perhaps the most important part of the gift.

The next step was to inform brother Alban, as he would inherit if the will failed. His solicitors replied that he had relinquished his rights in favour of Rosemary. She wanted to spend a few days at the Castle with her husband to have a look round. This was inconvenient and unnecessary but it could hardly be refused.

They had to doss down in Denys' flat, and one hopes they enjoyed their few days of feudal squalor. Rosemary was impressed with her possible inheritance, talked of how she would run it, and the profitability of cream teas. As they had nothing useful to do, Ruth suggested they might clean up the kitchen. They did this very thoroughly. We had not seen any sign of priceless relics amongst the rubbish. If there were, Ruth was really past caring about their fate.

By this time Ruth was beginning to recover from the general shock and despondency which had haunted her since Denys' death. She was preparing for another legal contest. Was there really an intestacy because the National Trust had refused the gift? In which case Rosemary would inherit as the next of kin. There could be another interpretation of the will – that cleverly worded will. The Castle had been left to the National Trust not outright, but as Trustees. A Trust does not necessarily fail simply for lack of trustees. It could be said that this was a play on words – the National Trust are trustees – trustees for the nation. Nevertheless the will named them as

Trustees. If the will was a valid one, if for instance there was a general charitable intention, other Trustees could be appointed. Ruth therefore decided to apply to the High Court for an interpretation of the will.

Forty-Five

The case would be heard in the Court of Chancery. This is an interesting procedure.

The parties involved bring their case before the Court, each setting out their interpretation of the facts, and the judge adjudicates. The parties are not fighting each other (well, not officially) there is no dramatic examination and cross-examination. The judge listens. He asks questions, may point out if an important point has been omitted, ask for instance if such and such a case has been considered. Then when both parties have finished explaining their case, the judge gives his decision.

In this case, the parties were Ruth, as executor of the will, maintaining that there was a general charitable intention; and Rosemary, claiming that Denys' sole wish was that the National Trust should have the property, and that as this was not possible, there was an intestacy, and she as next of kin should inherit.

A great deal of preparation had to be done – not only on the legal side, but also we had to obtain authoritative assessments about the historic and architectural merits of the Castle, the aesthetic and artistic value of the contents, and their general standing in the museum worlds, and also whether it was a viable proposition. For the law says you cannot dump a load of old junk on the Nation. There is a case on this. Of course the moot point is, what is a load of old junk? Some of the 'time capsules' recently gratefully accepted by the National Trust and reverently preserved would probably have been classified as such fifty years ago.

We had to get all the evidence together, calling on various experts. Our counsel, wishing to be helpful, suggested Lord Clark, then the television guru, as an impressive witness. We had to point out that the collections were not exactly his field. True, he had come to fame as a young man by his book on the Gothic revival, and the Castle might have interested him. However, we feared he would have regarded an approach as lese majeste.

In the end we consulted the author of 'Kent', in Pevsner's series on English counties. He had aroused Denys' eternal ire by referring to the Castle as 'stodgy'. He was very helpful when he made his inspection – said perhaps his statement had been a little too sweeping, but he did think the North front a little dull. Perhaps the Streatfeilds did too, because one of the 1836 'improvements' was the addition of the two towers flanking the north door; they are purely decorative. But with the present refurbishments, particularly of the surroundings, the North front has developed a certain austere dignity.

It was hard work but all very interesting, and we got to know many interesting people we might not otherwise have met. As I was retired I was free to go on all sorts of errands and do the massive secretarial work. The case did not come on until July 1979 so my enjoyment was spread over a long period.

Forty-Six

In the meantime we had to get on with clearing Denys' things at Chidd. He left a mountainous jumble of personal papers. He had kept everything – important and unimportant. Going through all someone's private papers is an unpleasant business, but one had a feeling he would not have minded. "These are records, mind you sort them carefully," one could almost hear him saying. Among the pieces of paper I picked up, carefully put into a little folder, was a five line note – in Charles II's own hand; the instructions to My Lord Treasurer to have the patent prepared for the dukedom to be conferred on the infant son of Louise de Kerouaille – the Duke of Richmond.

It was more like an academic exercise, a piece of research. Yet always at the back of our minds was a personal note. "Why, why, Denys? What made you tick? Is there no personal message for us? No explanation?..." We found none. I think perhaps there was none. Very likely he had no personal philosophy of life. Perhaps that is the case with many remarkable people. After their death, learned academics try to winkle out "the Truth", even devise theories into which they try to fit their subjects. But it is no good. You can never get to the heart of the matter because it has no heart. Denys was above all pragmatic. He took things as they came. Especially artistic objects. Collecting was his fanaticism. And that was a bond between us – for we were also collectors.

One thing about him we did learn.

He had, it appeared, been quite a lad in his time – from the day he left school. All his personal correspondence was there – not kept for any particular reason, I think. He just kept everything. He had some nice girls in tow at various times. There was Molly, a nurse – her photograph shows a pretty, thoughtful girl. As a nurse, she worried about his cough – quite rightly, it killed him in the end. She was frantic when, without any explanation, he failed to keep an assignment – the end of that romance. That was the curious thing – with two exceptions, he was always the one to break off a relationship.

Except in two cases – Margot, who broke off the engagement after two years because he would not name the day; and the fake countess. His anger with Margot, when she was soon afterwards swept off by an Army officer, was boundless; and this perhaps explains his capture by the Jewish Sylvia, whom he met afterwards. She wrote to him daily – wistful little letters hoping for a reply soon. One of them was not even opened. But she won – a victory she must have regretted.

We destroyed all the letters. We could not help feeling that he was a bit like Mr Doolittle – he did not intend to get 'ooked. A lot of men don't – in fact nowadays it seems to be a socially acceptable fact, but thirty or forty years ago it was not. Denys was just a bit before his time – as in other things.

We had to resume our weekly visits to Chidd. My mother rather resented this – but she enjoyed having tea with Tom, who always got his place specially tidy for her and kept a special china tea cup for her, with a rose on it.

The Vinsons were efficient, Ruth hoped they would stay. It would have been difficult to replace them at this juncture. They would have no additional help, though Ruth offered many times to try and arrange something. Mrs Vinson had two very charming sisters who came over regularly. Vinson thought a guard dog was desirable, so we got him an Alsatian through the police. From time to time dogs are offered to them, who though good, are not quite up to police training. Baron was one of those. He was a dear dog with a sense of humour. Vinson used to stroll round the grounds with him, looking masterful. Baron was a wonderful dog. If intruders appeared by the bridge in the north field he was after them in an instant. They went – you don't stop to argue with a dog like Baron.

The Vinsons were responsible for some 'improvements', notably the lining of the small Japanese room with wood, and painting the mahogony case black, which we were not sure about, but did not argue. They also had the concrete emplacement removed from the south front – they asked Ruth one week whether it should not be removed. She agreed, and next week it was gone. But they had taken away some good plants, particularly my rare little acer griseum, which was doing well. I was silently upset.

At last, early in June 1979, the case came up in Chancery. The judge was Mr Justice Oliver, who seemed very knowledgeable about the problems of country houses which were trying to earn their own living. In fact, some of his comments were so apt that we wondered whether he had ever been down to Chidd.

Our case was quickly presented. Then Rosemary's counsel rose. Having got on his feet, he stayed on them all day. He said he had nine points, which he submitted would show there was an intestacy, and therefore everything should go to Rosemary. His arguments were very learned and very complicated. I sat there baffled. I had qualified as a barrister many years before – though I had never practised – but this was all beyond me. One case he quoted was the 'old junk' authority, which I have mentioned previously; but whether he was inferring Chidd was old junk I could not quite make out. One argument he used was that Denys' sole intention was that the National Trust should take on Chidd and that was why he never mentioned any other charity. "He never thought they would turn it down," murmured the judge. "Would it not have been the same to him if the CPRE had been willing to take it?" Counsel claimed that Chidd was not viable because so far that year it had not produced enough income to cover expenses ... the judge remarked that major parts of income from visitors usually accrued during the Summer months, from July onwards.

Normally the judge enquires, if counsel is still speaking whether he is likely to finish within the next half hour because if so the Court will not interrupt him but sit late to allow him to finish his case. At 4pm promptly, Mr Justice Oliver rose, saying that the Court would adjourn until the next day. And, he hoped, Counsel would then elucidate his arguments. So far, whenever he tried to seize them, they eluded him like a bar of slippery soap. I felt comforted that the judge had been mystified too.

Next morning Counsel said he wished to make some clarifications, and eventually he summarised his nine points. We thought that the judge might reserve his decision, but he delivered his judgement at once; there was a general charitable intention in the will, and the Charity Commission was directed to set up a suitable arrangement for a Trust to be set up to run Chiddingstone, in accordance with DEB's wishes.

We had crossed one hurdle. At least Chiddingstone had a future to work for, though the distant scene was something we could not see, we could only go step by step. Ruth knew well what her task was: to see that the Castle remained a home, Denys' home, arranged as he left it, and to carry out the alterations and improvements which he had planned to make, but had not had the time or money to implement. Everything that was done must be of good quality, worthy of the house.

And what had to be done? The list was daunting. For nearly a hundred years the house had been allowed to deteriorate. The roof was leaking in forty places and rain came through to the ground floor. This meant that the place was perpetually damp. Countless repairs like rotten window frames, which let in the wind, minor things like missing door handles, brass replaced by plastic. The electricity system was dangerous, the water supply reluctant, the interior decoration dowdy, the upholstery shabby – there were few curtains. A new security system was needed. The collections were in need of advice on conservation. We were short of cash. We echoed the words of the love-sick girl in the Irish folk song: "Tis the want of money sure leaves me behind." At least the Castle had no debts. Ruth's careful accounting had seen to that.

The immediate problem was to bring in enough cash to keep the Castle going; and to get something done about the roof. Until this was watertight little could be done about redecorating the rooms.

To continue with the established system of staffing seemed the obvious thing to do: two resident couples who would live in the Castle all year round. For security reasons, it could never even for one instant be left unoccupied; and if you are going to call a place a 'home', people must actually live there. Otherwise it is a charade. In Denys' time, one couple had lived in the wooden lodge at the head of the drive, and another in an apartment in the north wing of the Castle. The second couple would now occupy Denys' old apartment in the south wing.

We could only pay a moderate salary, so we had to look for people with a pension in early retirement who wanted an interesting occupation for a year or two. These were awkward jobs to fill, for the actual hours worked were limited, but staff had to be present all the year, which was a tie. To make it worthwhile, you had to enjoy living in a large and historic house with its peace and spaciousness – it is a unique and pleasurable experience. For those accustomed to a suburban 'semi' the adjustment can be difficult. We had thought the prospect of free fishing might be attractive, but curiously, we never had a fisherman custodian.

The trouble was, this plan would obviously not appeal to the Vinsons. They preferred to work alone, as they had done since Denys' death. They had got on with him excellently, remembered him with affection, and it was understandable that such a break with the past would be distasteful to them. Nevertheless it was inevitable.

We did not want to lose them. They were responsible, knew the ropes, and were not afraid of emergencies. Even if they agreed unwillingly to accept a second couple, the position would be so unpleasant for the newcomers as to make their job untenable.

The difficulty resolved itself in a tragic manner. Mrs Vinson had suffered from asthma since she was a girl. She had a sudden attack and died a day or two later in hospital. Mr Vinson was devastated and left as soon as the replacement staff had arrived.

Forty-Seven

Keeping the Castle staffed was to prove a perpetual problem. We were fortunate in one of our early custodians – a retired police officer, an ex-detective. He taught us a great deal about the ways of thieves. We were naturally wary; listened to him, and remembered.

Then began a succession of custodians, good, bad, and indifferent. Mostly indifferent – how could they be otherwise? For the revival of Chiddingstone Castle was not their dream. They would never stay to see it accomplished. Indeed in their short sojourn they would hardly see any progress at all. Moreover the Castle, even though it had a bleak beauty, was an uncomfortable place, especially when repairs were going on.

It was an interesting experience, to see how people behave in their private lives. The Castle is quite a large place, and the apartments were not on top of each other, so there was no need for custodians to feel that they had no privacy. Yet some never tried to live in harmony. One of two only communicated by notes. Some of the men were inclined to be chauvinistic and proprietorial about their wife. "No one is going to tell her what to do" or "SHE is not going to do THAT."

Then there was the question of 'status'. We were to find if

we used the term senior or junior (in terms of service length) the 'seniors' tended to treat their colleagues like slaves. If no differentiating term were used, each tended to leave things to the other and no one took the initiative to report emergencies to Ruth.

The engagement of new custodians was a dreaded chore. It entailed much work – interviewing and correspondence, time which could have been spent on more productive activities. We never lacked applicants, and we went to such trouble to give adequate particulars and a good job specification; to point out the importance of working as a team. Sometimes we even asked the final applicants to spend a weekend at the Castle, to see what it was like. Yes, they said, they would love it, and longed to help.

Sometimes we wondered if they'd listened to us. It is a curious thing how people do not listen. They translate what one actually says into what they want to hear. Once at the Castle, they tended to develop a sort of '*folie de grandeur*', behaving as if they were Lords of the Manor. And then there were those who claimed to be 'sensitive', which meant they were apt to interpret the most chance remark as an insult to themselves, but had no conception that others had feelings.

The eighties were a dreadful decade for us, and looking back it is a marvel how we survived.

Forty-Eight

The other most urgent problem was the roof. Its appalling state threatened the safety and well-being of the whole building, and very little could be done to improve the interior – and so increase its attractiveness to visitors – until the structure was watertight.

The work had to be done out of season, so as to cause least disruption to the business of the Castle. Ruth had in mind that it should be done in three phases, north, east, and south roofs, and that it could be completed in three years. This was to prove a pipe-dream.

First, she had to find an architect who was used to working on ancient buildings, who thoroughly understood their problems; who could spot the sign of real trouble, but who could also appreciate when the damage was within the bounds of repair. Old buildings have remarkable resilience. This knowledge was specially important in the case of the Castle, because the 1805 alterations incorporated the remains of a previous building, and possibly one still older.

Most modern architects are not specialists in geriatrics. After making many enquiries Ruth was eventually put in touch with a surveyor who had experience of this type of work. We had a little money in hand from sales – the famous coffee pot for instance had to go – so work could be financed at once.

The surveyor introduced a builder who did immediate work on the gutters, and they held for a short time. On the roof, he suggested coating the slates with a sort of mastic. Now Ruth had read about this method of treating tiles and slates. It was relatively new then, but was already raising doubts. The slates and tiles were natural materials and could not breathe, and in the end disintegrated. When Ruth pointed this out to the surveyor, he said the process that he was suggesting was different. Still she hesitated. Just at this time she was introduced to an architect who was an outstanding expert. He confirmed that her misgivings were justified.

He offered to make a survey of the roof. He found that the work on the gutters was useless. The box gutters themselves were rotten, and must be renewed. The slates would all have to be renewed too. But apart from the roof, said the architect encouragingly, the Castle was in good structural condition. One could see what he meant. The stonework is of magnificent quality, and the mortar has stood up to two hundred years of wear remarkably. (The Castle architect, William Atkinson was a stickler for well-made mortar, and we probably have to thank him for a lot.)

The architect was well acquainted with English Heritage and he got their architect to come down in 1982 and inspect Chidd. He reckoned that the cost of repairs would be about £150,000, and that we would qualify for a grant. Those were the days of Dame Jennifer Jenkins, and it was said that some grants had been up to 75%. But she was to move on and English Heritage (i.e. the Government) became less generous.

We had the money to go ahead at once – a rare state of affairs, but somehow things just drifted on. Work did not begin until the Autumn of 1985. It was a fine October and we hopefully waited, week after week, for the builders to turn up.

By the time they did come, the weather had changed. We were in for a bad winter.

To save money, a temporary protective roof was not put up but the area was protected by a plastic covering. The wind was so strong one night that the cover blew off, and the rain poured into the building. The builders had to be sent for to rescue the covering. It was fortunate the Great Hall did not cave in.

By the late Spring the north roof was completed, and it looked really beautiful. The slates had been brought from a special quarry in Wales, and they were very much better quality than the original. We had a topping out ceremony in May 1986 and our patron Lady De La Warr officiated, gallantly climbing the tower and waving to us standing below. Inside, the attics were a scene of dereliction because there were no funds for the interior.

We waited for work to resume in the Autumn of 1986, but what with one delay and another, nothing happened until 1988. In the meantime, building costs were escalating. They were particularly high in the south east, and matters were made worse by the demand for building workers for the Channel Tunnel. Our savings were being devalued minute by minute. To crown everything, the beautiful new roof began to leak – over what used to be the billiard room in the tower. How the spirit of Mankelow must have laughed. "Told you so – you need basins!" But Mankelow's vast receptacles had been thrown away – we had nothing so effective.

The east roof, which had looked a less daunting proposition than the north roof, proved a nightmare. In the first place, we had to remove some defunct Victorian central heating pipes. The HSE said the lagging might contain blue asbestos and we must take all the official precautions. The old pipes were before the days of blue asbestos, but nevertheless we had to follow the rules. The lagging proved to be harmless, but the operation cost us five or six thousand, and worse still, several weeks delay.

When we did get started, it was found that the ends of the roof trusses were completely rotten and had to be treated. As they were concealed by the walls, this problem could not have been foreseen. The roof had to be supported on steel scaffolding, which went down to the cellars while the work was carried out. English Heritage at first jibbed at making a grant for all this extra work, which of course was not included in the estimate. But they relented in the end.

We only reached the final stages of the roof, the south wing, in 1990 – 91. There was unexpected difficulty here too. The mortar on the ornamental Gothic chimney was so worn away that the builders were faced with the problem of dismantling a pile of loose stones – very dangerous and they were reluctant to do it.

The cost of work on the chimney was considerable as new stone work had to be cut for it. There were complications with English Heritage about the grant, but they did finally help us. (The chimney was not Atkinson's work – how right he was about his mortar).

When the roof was completed in 1991 the cost had risen to £440,000. English Heritage made us a forty percent grant, the rest we raised ourselves, by sales, a legacy and gifts. It was a point we had hoped to reach in 1986. Only in 1991 could we really go ahead at speed with internal refurbishments – this, we hoped, would attract visitors, they could not go up to marvel at the roof.

Forty-Nine

Other invisible improvements had been going on, notably the rewiring. Defective wiring causes fires, and this has been the death of many a country house. Re-wiring a place like the Castle is not at all the same as rewiring a small villa. It is more like a hotel; and it is not a building which was ever designed for electric light. We found a marvellous electrician who understood the problem perfectly. From the beginning, the fuseboards were designed with the intention of taking the full load which would eventually be required for the Castle. The re-wiring was carried out stage by stage; at each stage provision was made for going on the next.

Last to be finished was the attic storey. The wiring here was so badly decayed that we had had the power cut off completely, until reparations could be made. I mention this work, because it is the sort of thing that visitors do not consider at all, as a major expense.

Like the water supply. That gave out completely one summer afternoon in 1980. The custodian had to hump pails of water from a standpipe near the garage to the cisterns of the loos. A first-aid operation to restore the supply cost us dear.

Only recently have we been able to finish the job Visitors cannot be expected, as they wash their hands, to reflect on the price it has cost us.

Fifty

At the time of Denys Bower's death the Castle attracted more than 30,000 visitors a year. It was one of the most successful of the smaller country houses. Yet we had no tearoom, no shop, the décor was flat though improving, and Denys did not go out of his way to welcome visitors, in fact very few knew him for the owner.

Why did they come? We watched them curiously. There were many whose one object seemed to be to walk through the place as briskly as possible. Once I stopped a young man in the Japanese room. "You have just walked straight past some of the loveliest lacquer without even looking at it. Stop, and let me explain what you should see and enjoy." He listened to me patiently, and at the end, smiled amiably, said: "I still don't like it." That is the trouble; most of the contents of the Castle are of an esoteric nature – though even English history seems beyond the horizon of many visitors. Sometimes they complained that things were not adequately labelled; but it is not just labelling that is needed, it is a whole education.

The truth is that many visitors came because there were so few places to go if you wanted a jaunt on Saturday or Sunday. We did our best to make Chidd more palatable. Some provision of refreshments was really essential, especially if we wanted to attract parties. During our first season the problem was solved when a local girl asked if she could rent the bungalow (then unoccupied) to do teas. Ruth thought this a good idea, but as it was a risky venture, offered the bungalow rent-free for the first season. One season was all it lasted. The young proprietress neglected to insist on payment, or at least a deposit in advance, on booked party teas. Several of them never came. The food was wasted. Bankruptcy.

We decided to organise things so that loss was impossible. We got together a scratch lot of equipment from around the Castle, gave the tea ourselves, and brought over a weekly supply of home-made biscuits. That was all we sold. At the end of the season we had made quite a good profit. We ploughed this back, and after several years were about to offer quite a pretty little tearoom. For parties, we bought in food from a caterer. The difficulty was restraining over-enthusiastic custodians who wanted to branch out too freely. It is quite impossible to estimate what demand will be on any particular day, and we simply could not afford to over-cater.

The phenomenon of the shop in country houses is odd. It began, presumably, with pure souvenirs, and then extended to all kinds of things, not related to the house at all. Supplying these shops is now a business, but finding suitable and marketable stock is difficult. Many suppliers will only sell in minimum quantities, too large for the small shop. The less you can buy, the higher rate you pay, and therefore the less profit on your sales. Really, the shop is not a viable proposition unless you have at least sixty thousand visitors a year. But visitors now expect it, and we keep it as part of the show. Children are excellent customers, but their parents are feeling the pinch of the depression. Ten years ago we could sell things fairly readily up to £10. Now we are lucky to get £3, though we have some good bargains.

In spite of these little amenities, numbers continued to

drop. We decided to concentrate on children. Education was the gimmick of the early eighties.

One custodian had been a teacher. He was very enthusiastic; organised a wine and cheese party for local teachers, when he explained what we could offer. They had a happy time, went away, and we never saw them again. I wrote a personal letter to all local head teachers, not a single reply.

Ruth and I went to a seminar on educational projects, and Ruth commissioned a package on Ancient Egypt. It was not very inspired; we felt we could have done better ourselves. Over the years we have had only a few schools, until a year or two back when the collections were mentioned on television. Our young visitors have been primary school children, very well-behaved and eager. A persistent comment on Chidd is interesting: they like it because they say it is so quiet. Small children are often bewildered by noise and hassle.

Numbers continued to fall alarmingly. We were facing several adverse factors. Other activities, such as theme parks were becoming available. This was what many of our visitors really wanted. The truth is that Chiddingstone is not what is called a 'tourist attraction'. That is, it is not a commercial organisation whose only object is to make a profit by entertaining people; and if it fails in this it goes out of business. True, we hope visitors will enjoy themselves at Chidd, but the prime object of the collections is not entertainment but enlightenment. To try and turn it into a half-hearted theme park would destroy it.

It was evident that individual visitors were not enough support for the Castle. We must turn to other means.

We reflected that the Castle was once the centre of local entertainment – garden parties, tennis, cricket, dances – could it not be used again for occasions which, in scale and type, might have taken place there in its private days?

So, what about wedding receptions? The Trustees agreed that the grounds should be made available for hire as a site for marquees for wedding receptions and other suitable functions. This proved very popular. It was a sure way of bringing in an income – we always insisted on payment in advance. The Castle was closed to visitors on such occasions, so the guests had the place to themselves. As a result, we had an enquiry from a leisure activities firm, who arranged staff dances and other festivities for commercial firms.

We stipulated that the music must be kept quiet – no BEAT. We looked in at the first dance, to make sure that things were under control. The house is not, unlike many country houses, situated in the middle of nowhere, but in a village; we have to be very careful not to annoy neighbours.

Hardly a sound could be heard outside the marquee. Inside, the dancers were sitting quietly, the men down one side of the marquee, the girls down the other, eying each other gloomily. Only one or two daring couples had taken to the floor. Maybe you do need drink, drugs and the BEAT to get people really worked up. Nevertheless the neighbours still complained, so next time we went round with a noise meter. We had difficulty in getting any recording at all. However there were no more dances, so the problem solved itself.

Another possibility presented itself. A craft fair organiser wanted to hire the grounds for three days for a craft fair. Now craft fairs were becoming very popular in the eighties,; there really were quite a number of skilled craftspeople about. The Trust agreed to a marquee in the grounds. But when we arrived to make a tour of inspection on the first morning, we found the organiser had misinterpreted the terms of her contract. She had let spaces for stalls inside the Castle as well; in fact, it was crammed with them.

Ruth decided to let matters proceed. We needed the hiring fee badly. Unfortunately for the next three days it rained solidly. The fair had been well publicised, and for three days visitors poured into the Castle continuously, their shoes well coated with Wadhurst clay. The Castle's treasures had never exerted any such attraction.

The custodians did a magnificent job clearing up the mess. No more craft fairs – that was another activity crossed from our list.

Yet another possibility, clay pigeon shooting, an activity then in its infancy. Our clay pigeon shoots were very high class affairs, organised by a very gentlemanly firm for very important people. It seemed this was just the sort of activity the Castle was made for. It had been a great shooting estate, and Lord Astor of Hever had retained his shooting rights over it until the late '60's. The shoots were arranged in a secluded spot, the public being of course entirely excluded on those days. All went well at first, but one day the marksmen nearly got more than they bargained for. Just as they were raising their guns, an irascible elderly neighbour appeared right in the line of fire, waving his arms in fury. He was led away gently; he made his way back in by an unauthorised back entrance. I think this little incident rather put off the organiser. There were no more shoots, and we were glad, for the trees and shrubs were being shot to pieces.

Then, in 1987 – 88 the Trust undertook a vast exercise, as hosts to the National Westminster Bank for a staff training course lasting six months. One hundred and fifty staff a day attended, and the training being carried out in a special building – a semi-permanent structure known as the SPS, a completely new conception. It was to be erected discreetly out of public sight on the south field. The trainees would take their lunch – provided by us – in the Castle. The SPS was to be built on concrete pylons, but owing to extensive rain, the ground was so waterlogged that they kept sinking. Then came the 1987 hurricane. The builders were desperate. Could they not have a site with a hard bottom? The car park would be excellent.

This meant getting special planning permission, which

was obtained – not without resistance from some neighbours. The SPS would be publicly visible, but it would only be there for 6 months.

The strain on the Castle of such heavy and persistent use was terrible. In April it emerged battered and more dilapidated than ever. But the exercise had been very profitable, and the money was needed to help pay those ever escalating costs for the repair of the roof. We still find mementoes of the occasion. When working in the wood by the orangery some time ago we came upon some miniature monoliths just below ground. What could they be? Relics of antiquity? Suddenly we realised: the pylons from the south site, which the builders were to dig up and take away. They had not taken them very far.

Our next experiment was a short affair – a 'family day' for a large company. One of the archers shot himself in the foot, but otherwise it was a peaceful occasion, and so successful that another company asked us to prepare a programme for a similar event for them. Before we had got very far they cancelled the commission – the depression had begun to take shape.

This also was the fate of another developing activity of which we had great hopes. A large car manufacturer held a promotion of their new models in the grounds, for which they are ideally suited. Another company consulted us, and we were on the point of clinching a deal when their annual report came out. We read it with dismay – and so apparently did they, for the negotiations were cancelled at once. I suppose we should have been bold and pointed out to them that the promotion was just what they needed.

Restricted though we were, we did try to improve the Castle amenities. We made a dining room out of the 17th century kitchen in the old domestic quarters. It had been stripped of all its interesting features, but on an inspired guess we had the old fireplace opened up – no one had suspected its existence. As a result the room was cured of its perpetual dampness. Experts had advised electro osmosis or the provision of a damp proof course.

A major work was the conversion of the ruinous butler's wing to a conference centre. Constructed c1893 it runs across the north side of the courtyard, uniting the former dining room with the coach house. It had to be reroofed and one wall rebuilt, but internally it still retained its panelling of matchboard. We kept this because we thought it had a pleasant rustic feeling. Then a friend brought down someone who is an expert in these things to advise us on how to set about marketing it. He was very kind, but we could see that he did not think that rusticity would have any appeal to a plushy business community.

We did not hesitate. The matchboard was ripped out, the ceiling plastered, and bordered with the most beautiful and horribly expensive Georgian Gothic moulding we could find. The most fastidious taste could not fault it. I took great pains over the curtains, though they were a disappointment – I never liked them. But alas, the bottom had dropped out of the lucrative market. Business no longer had excess money to spend. It was some time before there was any interest – and then it came from an unexpected quarter: the Continent.

I made curtains for all the other rooms in the Castle too, to try to cheer things up a little. It was a difficult task because it is hard to handle a twelve foot double width curtain unless you have a proper workroom. I could not face interlining, so they hung in rather a dejected way; especially when they were soaked by the incoming rain, which happened too often.

Fifty-One

By 1989 the reparations to the roof had reached a stage where it was possible to set about internal redecoration. The attic billiard room seemed to have dried out, though rain had come into the conference centre almost as soon as it was finished, and spoilt a section of the Gothic moulding.

The north hall, staircase and drawing room were redecorated. They were done to the highest quality. But one of the problems was draperies. The drawing room must now have curtains. We did not seek a reproduction of a late Georgian material and style. The room had never been a setpiece, like a décor designed by Adam. It had changed gradually over the years, though the present furnishings and pictures could in fact have been there in 1800. What we needed was something sympathetic and in character. But good curtains are extremely expensive. They are individually designed, hand made – and they give an air of distinction and elegance to a room as nothing else can. They were simply beyond me.

Then I had an idea. Why should not someone sponsor our curtains? Everyone seemed to have sponsors. Why not us? Some textile manufacturer might help, but it was no use writing in a general way to the Chairman, one must know whom to approach.

At that time there was in Ticehurst where I live, a firm of interior decorators – Howard Charles – a curious firm to find in a village, for they have Mayfair standards. (They are now in Tenterden). I knew Howard and Catherine Grimmette quite well, so I asked what they thought of my idea, and if it was any good, who were the people to approach.

They thought it worth trying, gave me some names, and Catherine said that if I were successful she would make the curtains, which was very sporting of her.

The only positive response was from Warners. They could not – for business reasons – give us the material, but would let us have it at a nominal fee of £1 a yard. This was generosity indeed, for we would need about forty yards for the set of curtains. We chose a most beautiful glazed chintz. The room looked lovely when finished – the first instalment of the recovery of a great house. Catherine later rehung all of the ground floor rooms, and I think I may safely say that no country house in the country has finer curtains.

We also decided to re-orientate the visitors circuit of the Castle – to bring it in at the south instead of the east. It was something Denys Bower had always wanted to do, but had never had the means of bringing into effect. Visitors could now enter via the restored Well tower, across the little courtyard, past the old kitchens and into the south entrance and the Castle proper. The 1805 kitchen still has a good many of its original fittings, and restoration revealed over the fireplace a curious door which opens horizontally and gives access to a little cupboard over the fire – a fuel store possibly, but it is unique. By coming in this way, visitors could see the whole of the Castle, and some interesting domestic history. We had great difficulty in educating custodians to this new circuit. They had a tendency to open the great south doors which creates a draught right through the Castle.

Now we felt we could embark on some publicity for the Castle. Hitherto any 'puffing' would have probably resulted in disappointed visitors, and spoilt chances for the future. We wondered if we could tap the Japanese market, so I wrote to the leading Japanese tourist agencies pointing out all we had to offer to their customers. They replied courteously but evasively; all except one, who invited us to go and see him, and he would explain the Japanese market.

It was an interesting but discouraging experience. Mass tourism, he explained, was a phenomenon of prosperity in Japan. For the first time many Japanese in modest circumstances found a lifetime ambition within their reach, a visit to Europe. And it was just that: as many countries as possible crammed into a fortnight. The Japanese we saw milling around London were probably on a two day visit. They might see the Tower, Stratford upon Avon, but certainly not Chiddingstone Castle. Some wealthier Japanese were beginning to come a second and third time; there might be some hope with them. But, he said, the Japanese were always impressed by a prestigious visitor. Try and persuade an important Japanese to visit the Castle and so encourage his compatriots.

We went away and pondered over this. The most important Japanese? Why the Ambassador of course. Desperation makes one bold, so I simply rang up the Embassy, asked for the Ambassador's secretary, was put straight through to her, to my amazement, and explained my mission. The secretary was very courteous. Could I send details – she thought their information was out of date. She thought the Ambassador would be very interested; and so he proved to be. In a few weeks arrangements were made for His Excellency Ambassador Chibha and Mme Chibha to pay an informal visit to Chiddingstone Castle.

They were both charming. Bill Tilley (W H Tilley one of our Trustees) was there to welcome them. He was an expert on

Japanese swords and lacquer, of international fame. The only westerner to be honoured by Token Kenkyu Rengokai – the Japanese Sword Study Unified Association – which presented him with a Certificate of Appreciation.

He demonstrated one of our finest swords to the Ambassador. It was a delightful visit. Knowing of the Japanese reverence for protocol we had been rather apprehensive – might we unwittingly do the wrong thing? But all was straightforward, and I sometimes wonder if it would be as easy to approach that citadel of informal democracy, the US Embassy.

Ambassador Chibha returned to Japan shortly afterwards, so he never came up to Chiddingstone again. We never were able to penetrate the Japanese business community, or make any regular contact with the Japanese at all. We had thought that ex-patriates might like their children to see some of the wonders of old Japan, but it is a hard trail to follow, and we have too often been prevented from following up constructive progress by the pressure of mundane troubles.

Bill Tilley was always a help – and inspiration. He adored Chiddingstone and gave it real practical help, especially in raising money. Denys Bower had left what was called a reserve collection of swords, which had never been part of the main collection, to be sold to raise money for the restoration of the Castle. Bill advised on the prices these should fetch, and which should be retained if at all possible, on account of their unique quality. He also knew how to clean up the swords, a very rare skill. He had remarked that Denys Bower was the modern reincarnation of William Beckford – he wrote an article for *Country Life* on the romantic image of Beckford and Denys Bower – he was outraged because *Country Life* edited it without his knowledge or permission, but we thought it read very well all the same.

Bill used to call Denys Bower 'Our Unique Selling Product', and said we must make more use of him. We thought about this, and were considering whether we could recreate his sitting room, or study, in some part of the Castle, when we had an unexpected offer from the National Trust.

The National Trust were willing to send their experts round the Castle to advise us generally on what we should do to improve our prospects. Now many people had given us advice, it is the one thing that people will give freely, but this was different advice from a body which really understood our problems, knew what was feasible for us and what not. They had been through it all themselves. We told them about our idea and our USP. They said it was excellent, but we had chosen quite the wrong place for the room. It must be the first room the visitors enter, and it must make an impact which will remain with them all through their visit. We recognised the truth of this at once. We knew which room it must be: the library which almost exactly faces the entrance door. It was too small for the books, which were overflowing all over the place, and very dilapidated – part of the ceiling had come down when an over-enthusiastic plumber was working on the floor above. The room exactly above was Denys' old study – the library was the same shape and size – ideal. We also had the ideal room for the library, the old billiard room on the second floor. The only problem was, how to move 3,000 books up two floors by a winding staircase from the south to the north front. Four volunteers came forward. They would take the books up, a cardboard box load at a time, as soon as the new library was redecorated and ready.

This offer was gratefully accepted. The library was prepared, two antique glazed bookcases restored and new ones made. Then the move began, and went on for several weeks. Bill helped to sort the books as they came up. In the end there were sufficient books to fill the new library entirely (and it alone was much larger than the old one) and a new reading room next door. It looked perfect – a real library at last. But not for long. There was a bad storm some time later on.

Fortuitously, the custodians thought fit to make a tour of the second floor. The water was pouring into the library. They pulled the books to safety – fortunately they had been preserved by the bookcases, and rang us up to ask what to do with a load of damp books. Luckily I knew something about this from my book-binding courses, and was able to advise. No one has yet found out WHY the water came in, and continues to do so.

The reincarnation of Denys Bower's study was an unqualified success. Somehow it gave significance to the whole place. It looked imposing. Catherine Grimmette made some magnificent yellow curtains for it, the old Regency damask being in rags again. Visitors were interested in Denys Bower – and amazed by his achievement. Their numbers did not increase – but they ceased to fall – and those who did come were enthusiastic.

It had been Bill Tilley's ambition to write a definitive catalogue of the lacquer and swords, but he was never to accomplish it. He died in January 1993, an irreparable loss as Trustee and friend. He had been terminally ill for some time, and in much pain, yet up to his death he was coming about the Castle. His ashes were scattered in the grounds as he had wished. His gentle spirit is in good company with Denys.

Fifty-Two

Ruth and I had just come back from holiday in May 1993. She had been going through the post when she came to me almost laughing. She said, "I thought this thing was a spoof at first, but it really is official paper." She handed me the letter, which informed her that she had been awarded an MBE in the Birthday Honours List for her services to the restoration of Chiddingstone Castle. What puzzled us both, was who could have put her name forward? It must have been someone with influence, because these honours are not given easily. It was common knowledge that she was Managing Trustee, and had many responsibilities, but no one knew just how much she did – except the other Trustees, and they knew nothing about the award. No honour was more deserved – but who was it that saw those deserts were honoured? That is a mystery still.

It was the Prince of Wales who officiated at the ceremony at Buckingham Palace early in November. This was the culmination of Ruth's happiness, for she has the greatest admiration for the Prince and his tireless work for conservation. I was present, with a friend who has done much for Chidd, and had a very good view of the Prince. We were struck by his charm of manner, his interest in those who were being honoured, and his concern for some who were infirm. He takes longer over the ceremony than the Queen, and Ruth had a chance to tell him briefly about Chidd. The whole ceremony was very impressive and haunting.

We did not know that the ceremony was being recorded as part of the film, 'A Year in the Life of the Prince of Wales'. When we saw the film we realised that this was Ruth's ceremony and I said, "I don't expect we shall see you," and the next thing we knew she was walking across the screen.

Epilogue

It is forty years this Whitsun since Chiddingstone Castle was opened to the public by Denys Bower. He was in desperate financial straits. He owed the Bank the whole purchase price of the Castle, and the interest on the loan was piling up remorselessly, with no income to repay it. The Castle was in bad structural and decorative repair. He was plagued by other debts. But he had one solace – his Countess, his fake countess. She stood between him and reality. All through the summer of 1956 and 1957, he could dream of his future bride and helpmate. Then quite suddenly, and for no reason that he could understand, his support disappeared. Why? Perhaps she saw the financial debacle ahead, and wanted to leave the sinking ship in time; perhaps she was a gold-digger who saw there was no gold; perhaps she was just tired of the charade and did not imagine that anyone could take her so seriously. Anyway, he was brought face to face with a bleak and lonely future. The irony of the situation is that if his foolish behaviour had not led to the shooting incident, if he had not been accused, found guilty and given the most appallingly unfair sentence, he would indeed have had no future. The Castle and his collections would have been sold, there would have been little left for him to live on, and with his lifework destroyed, he might indeed have attempted suicide – and this time successfully.

As it was, after four years in prison and time for reflection, the Almighty may have decided that he had been punished enough for mere foolishness (which is often paid for as dearly as sin) and brought to his aid the only person who could save him. It was an incredible conjunction of circumstances. After Denys' death, his friend Grant Uden was to say that he regarded us as his family, and that gave him the support he needed. True, he did not always treat us as well as he should have done, but that is what families are for. The prodigal is always welcome home.

He knew that Ruth had great respect for his artistic judgement. She never troubled him about his private whims. He knew her devotion to Chidd was as fanatical as his, and possibly more dogged, and it was a grateful gesture on his part to follow her advice on its ultimate disposition. He knew I think, that the National Trust might well refuse it, and that if they did so, its fate was in Ruth's hands, his sole executor – it could not have a more determined or loving protector.

Milton Keynes UK
Ingram Content Group UK Ltd.
UKHW030954020924
447770UK00005B/337